"To those who shared their knowledge, experiences, and wisdom with me, my sincere gratitude for enriching this book with your collaboration."

Bruno Baldaccim

This Book Belongs to:

○────────────────────○

Test Color Page

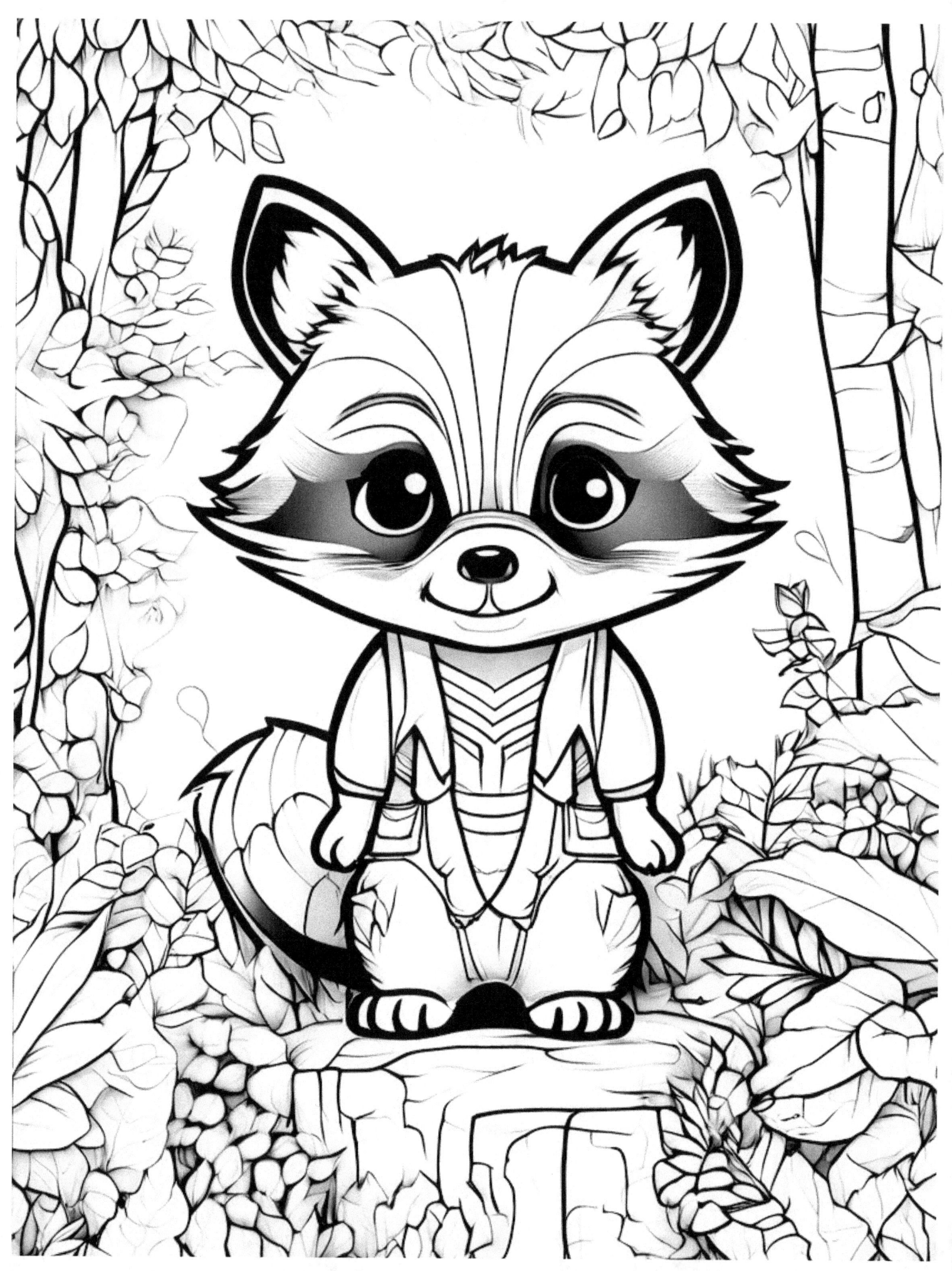

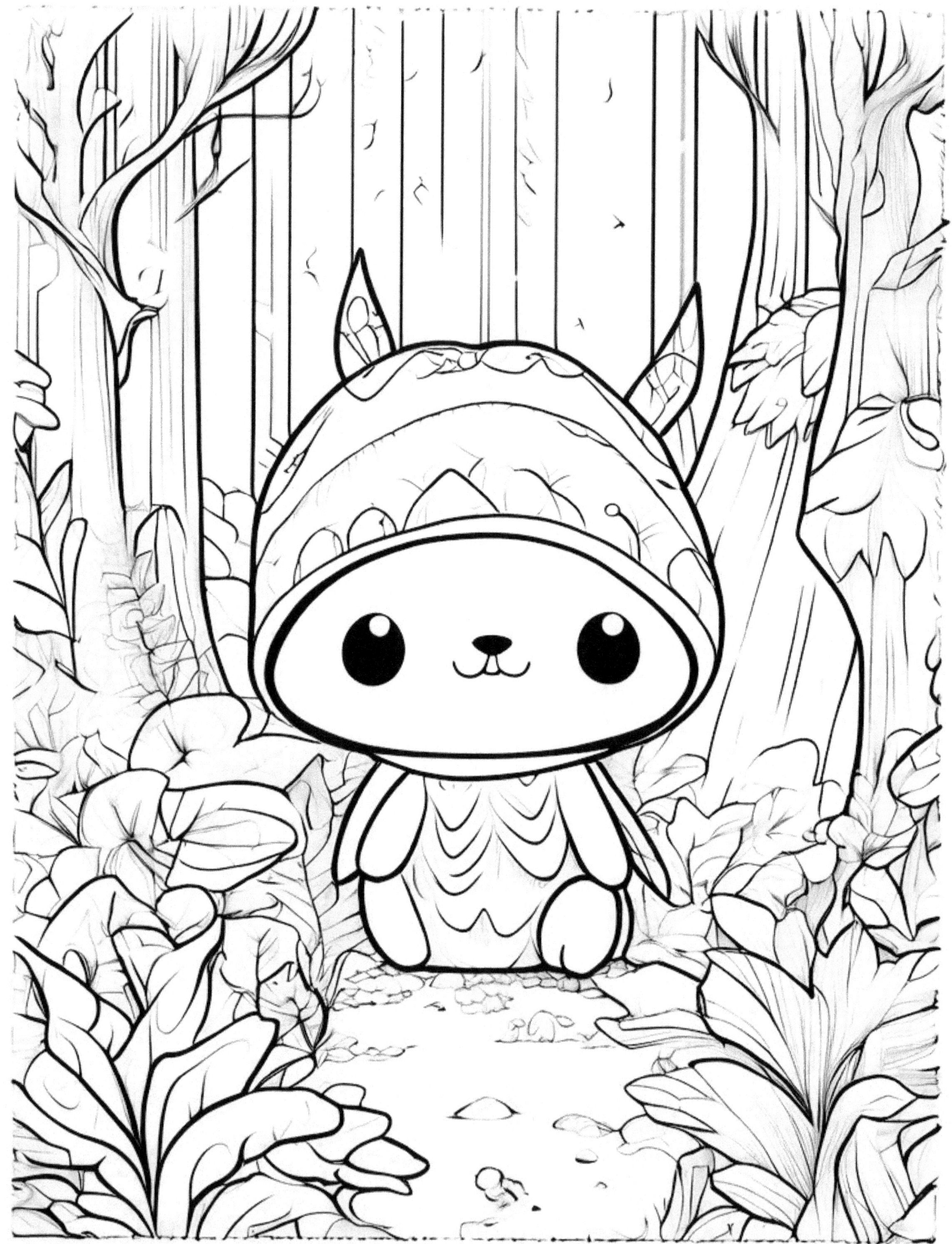

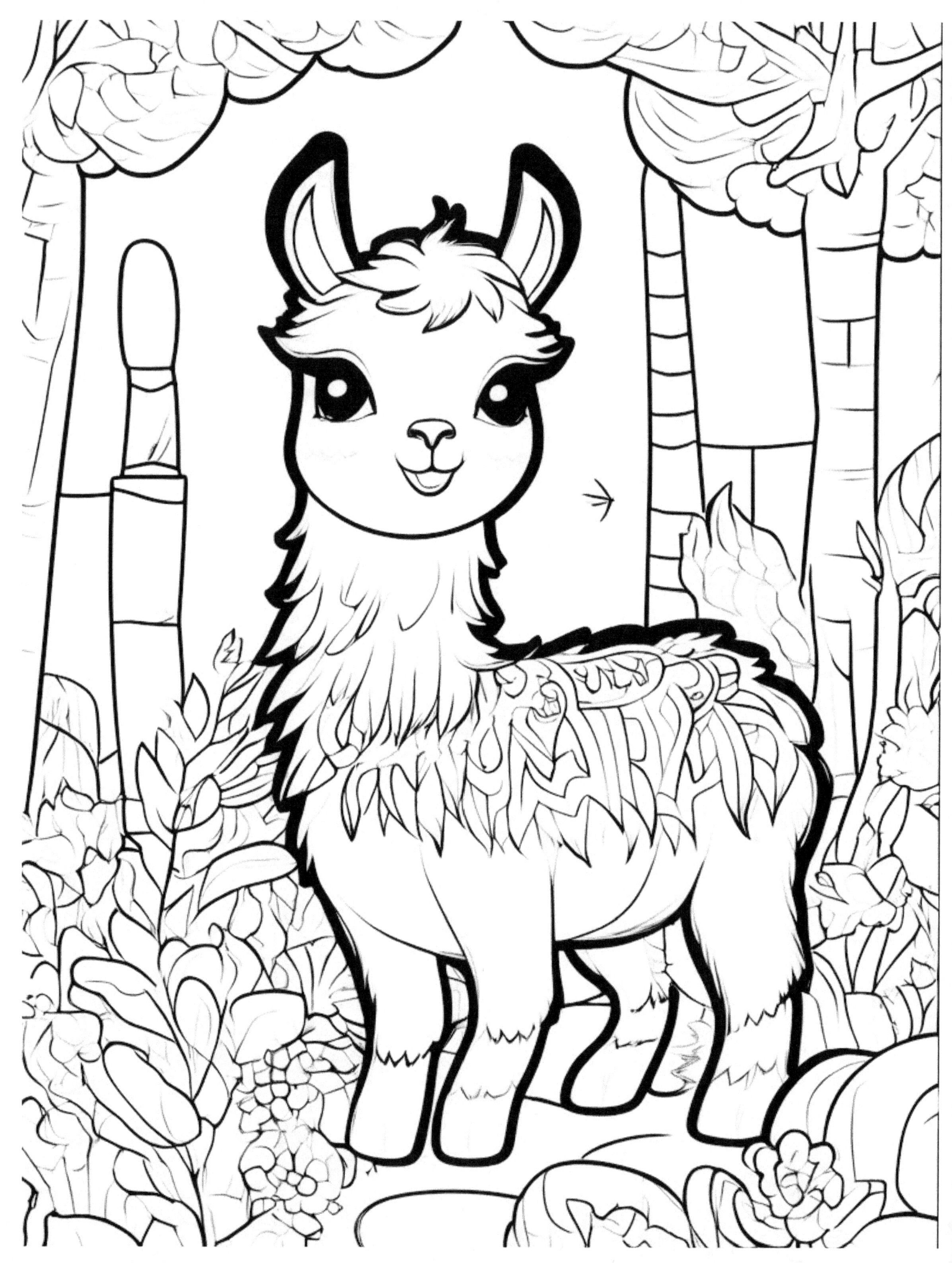

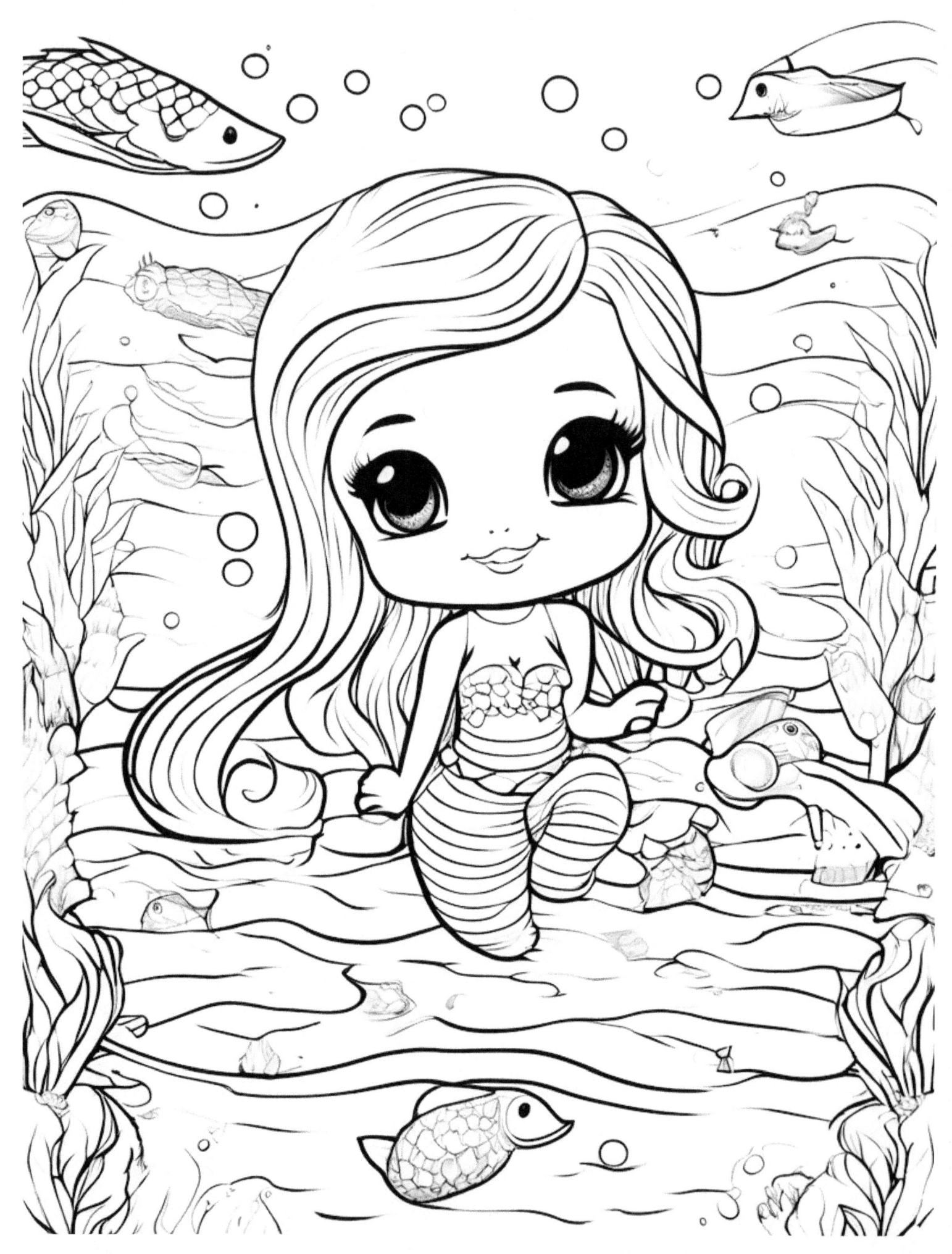

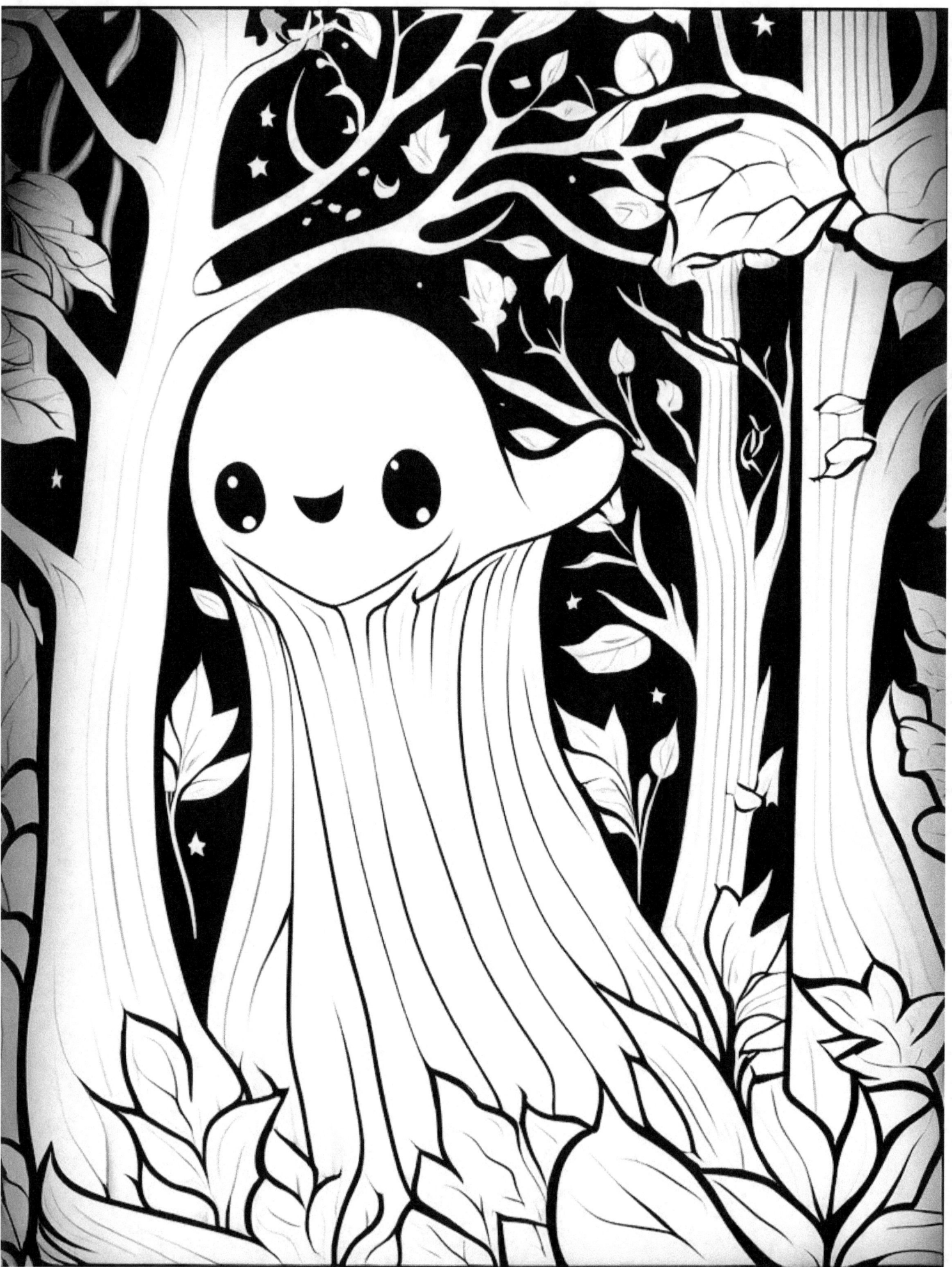

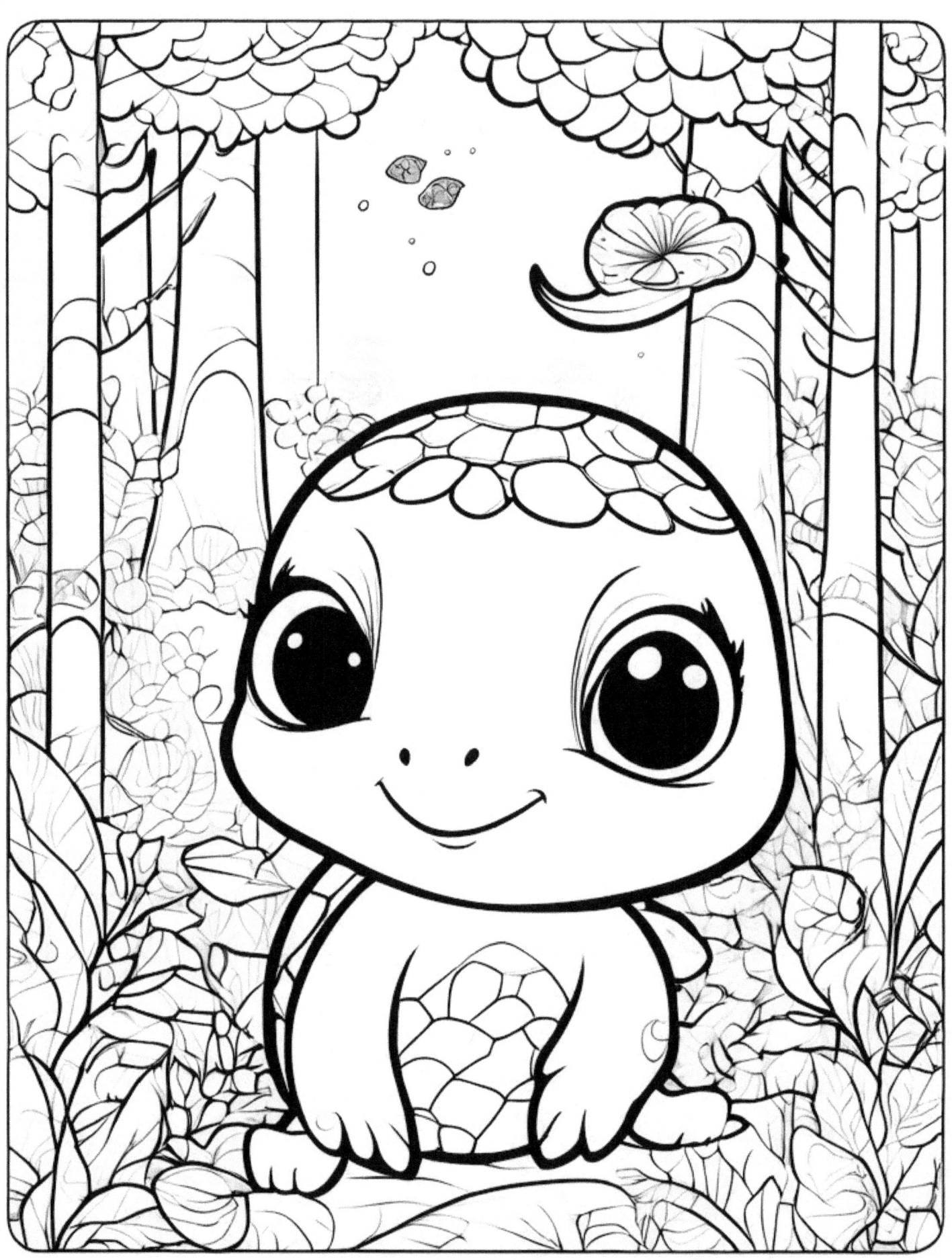

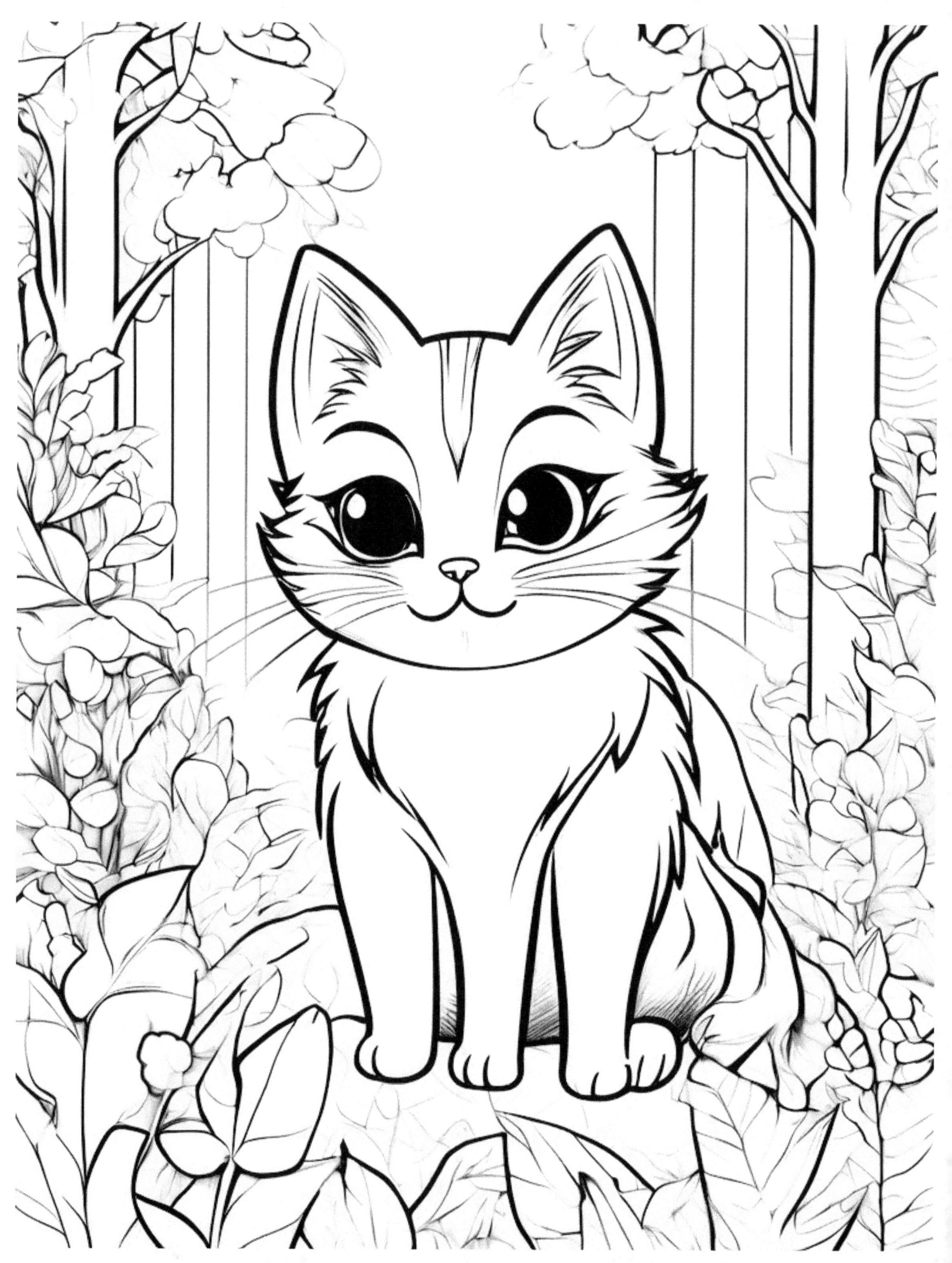

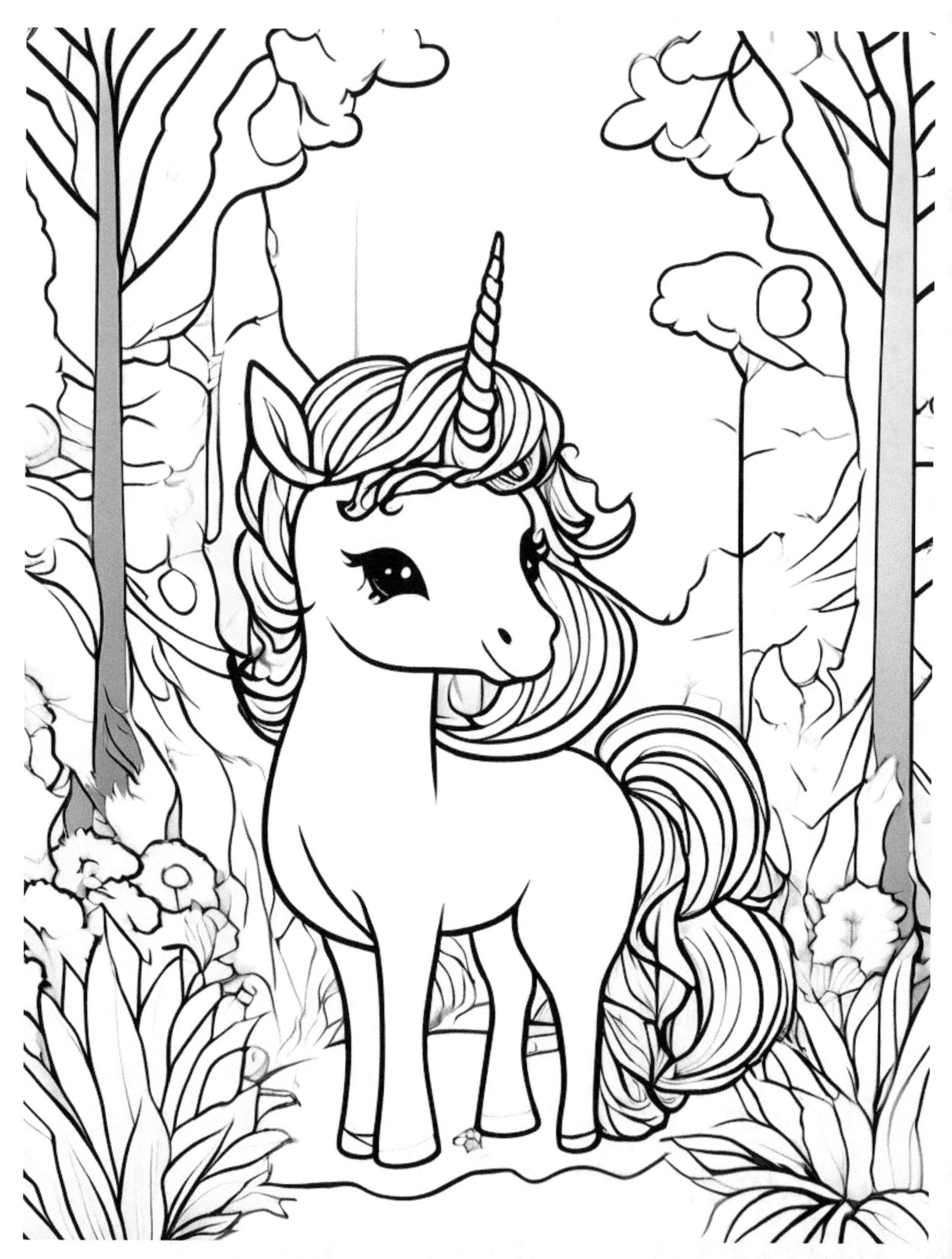

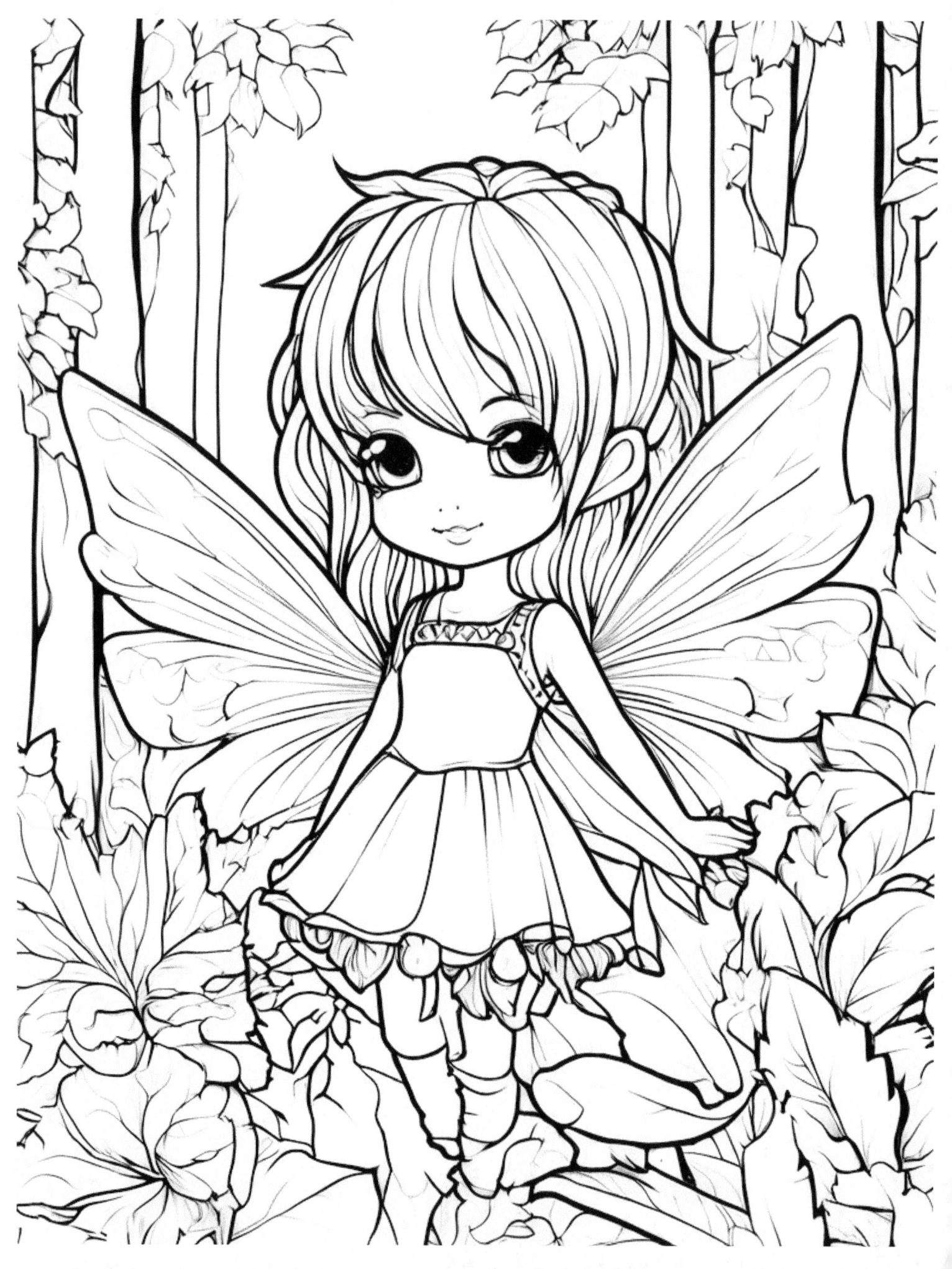

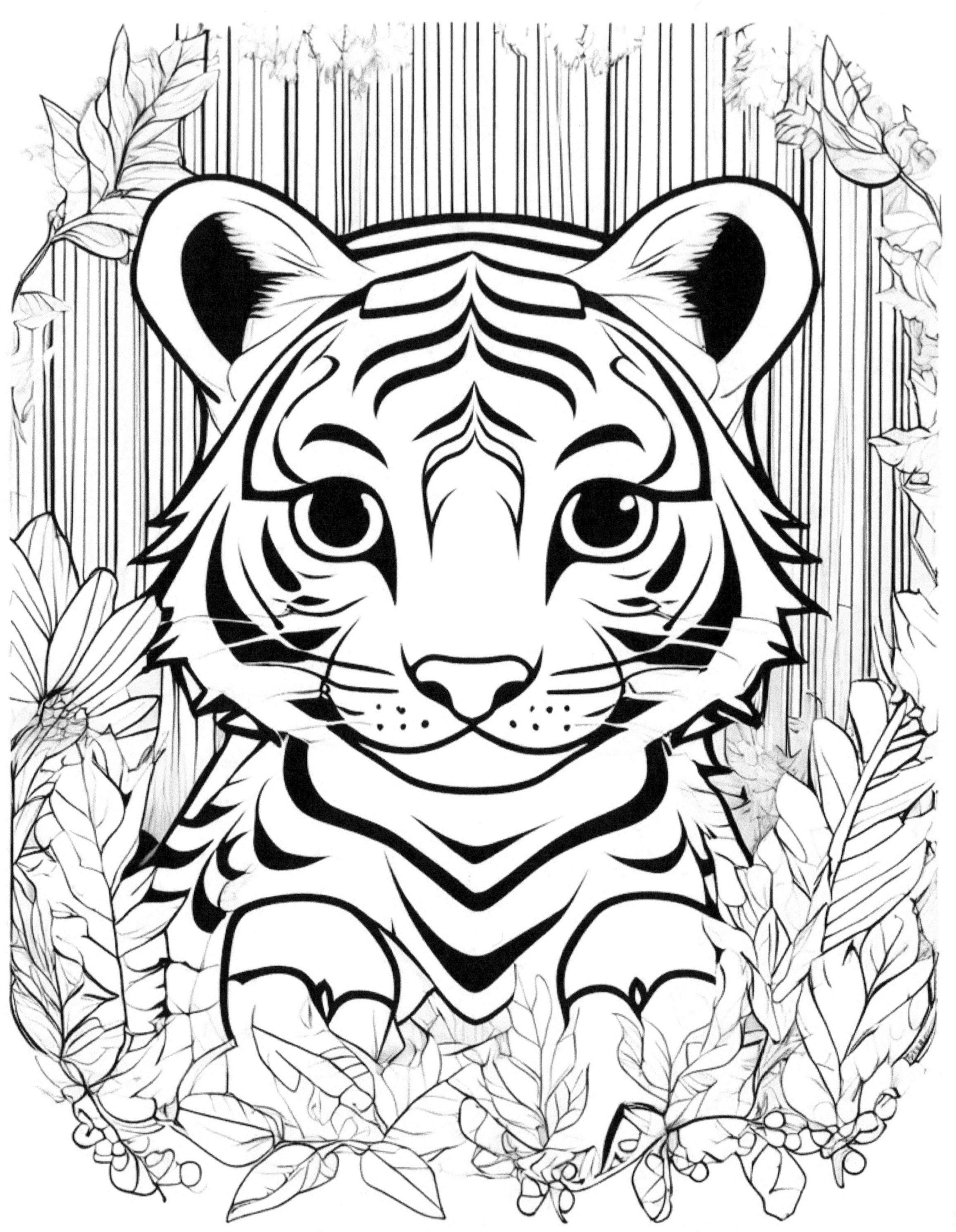

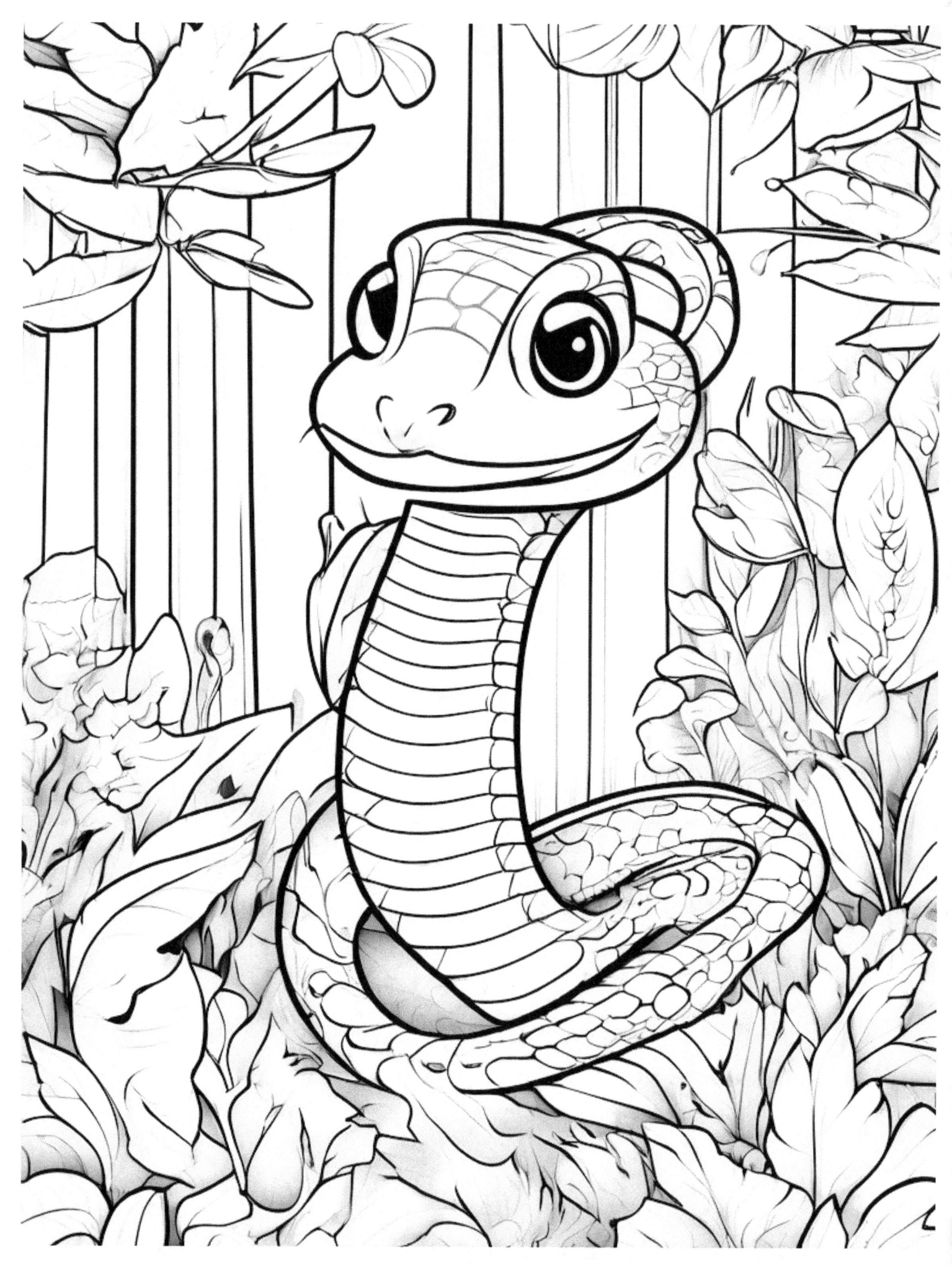

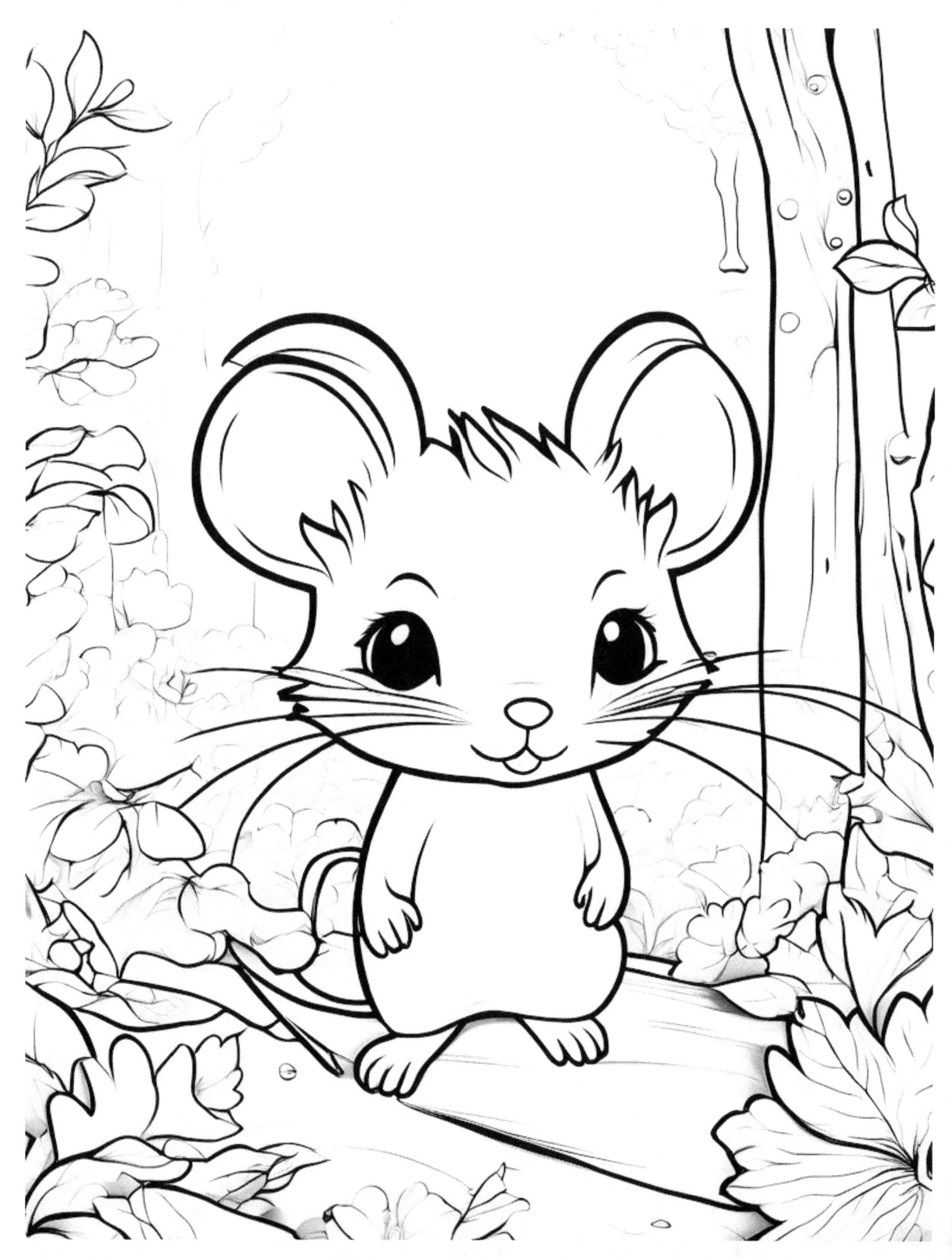

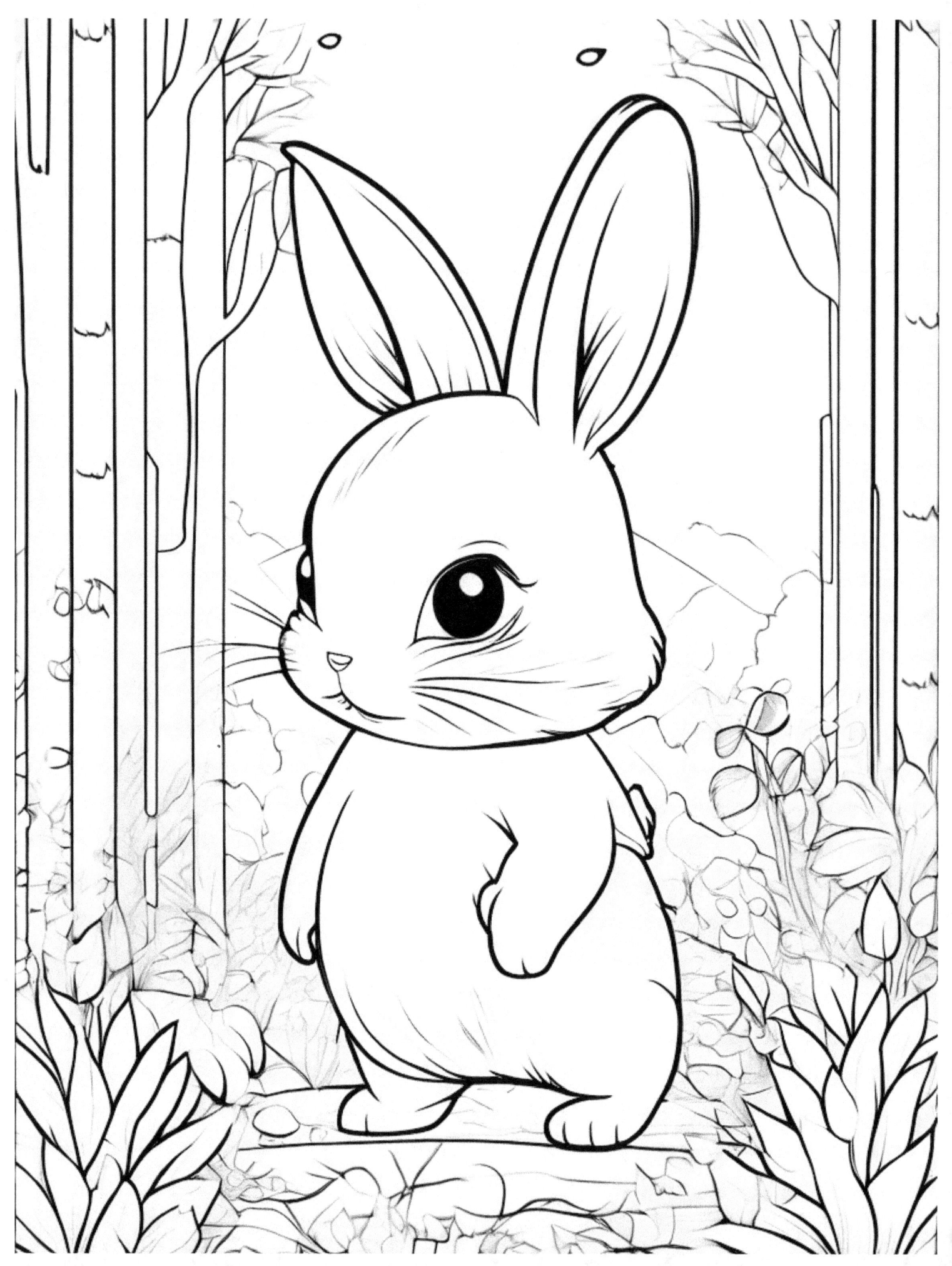

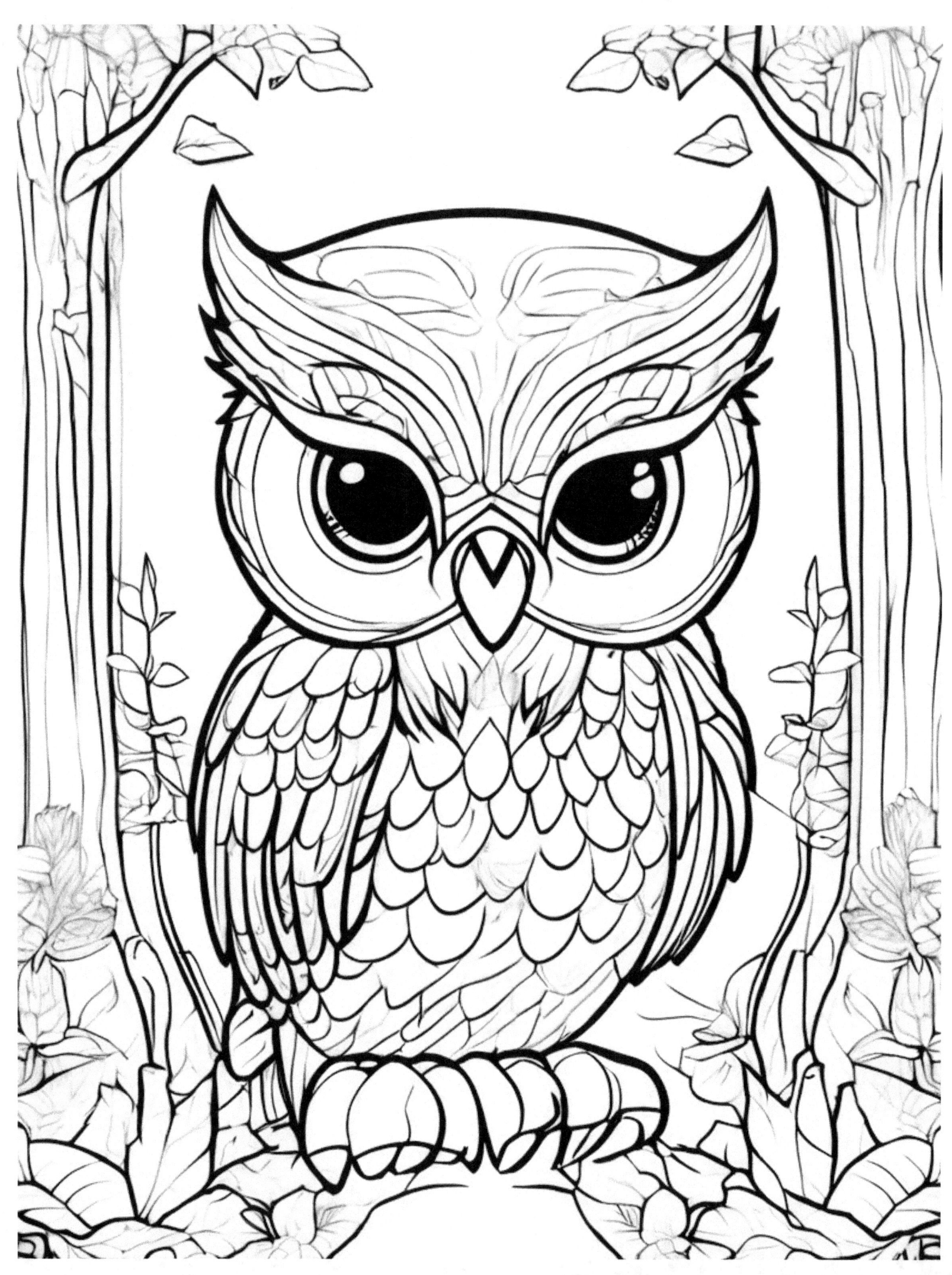

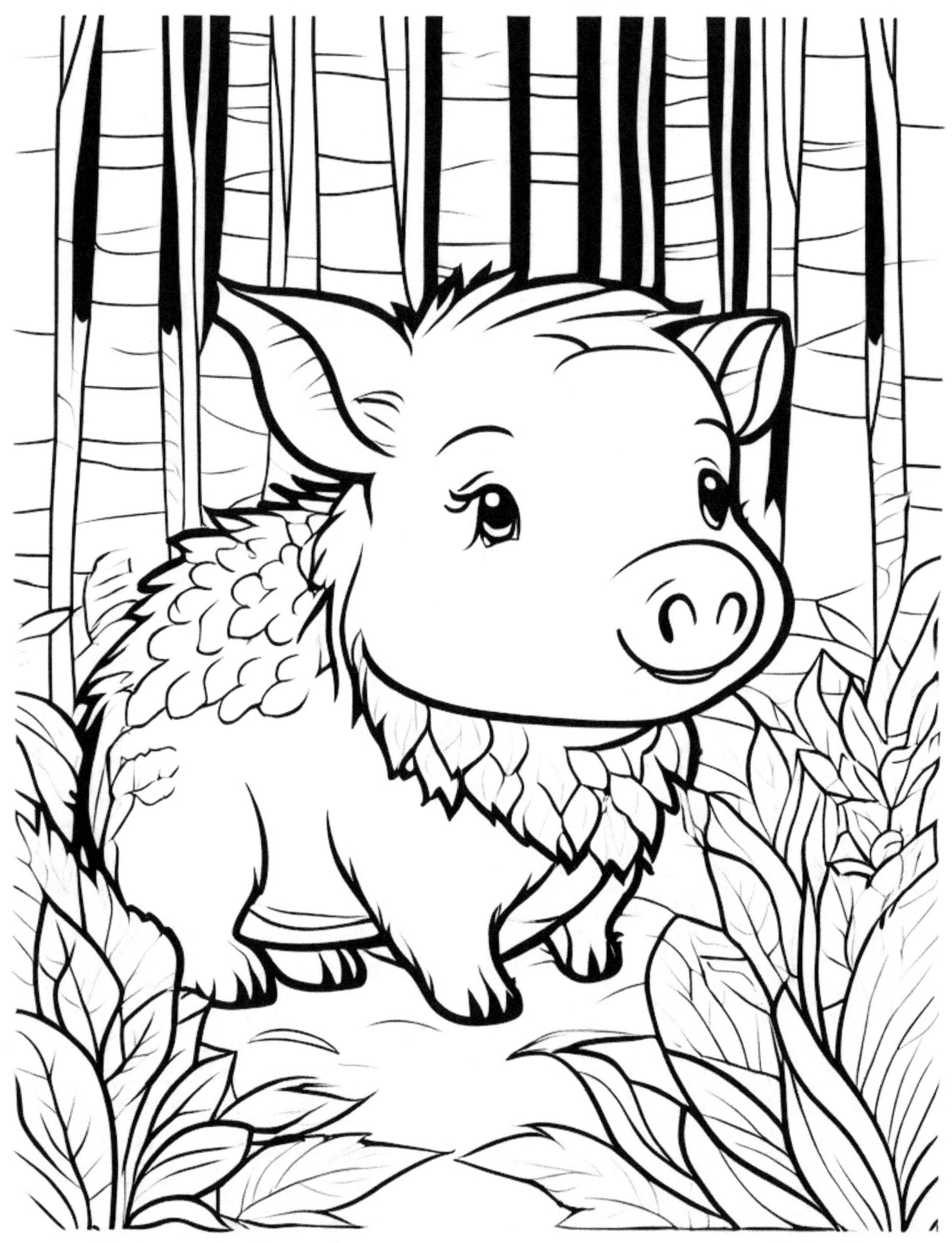

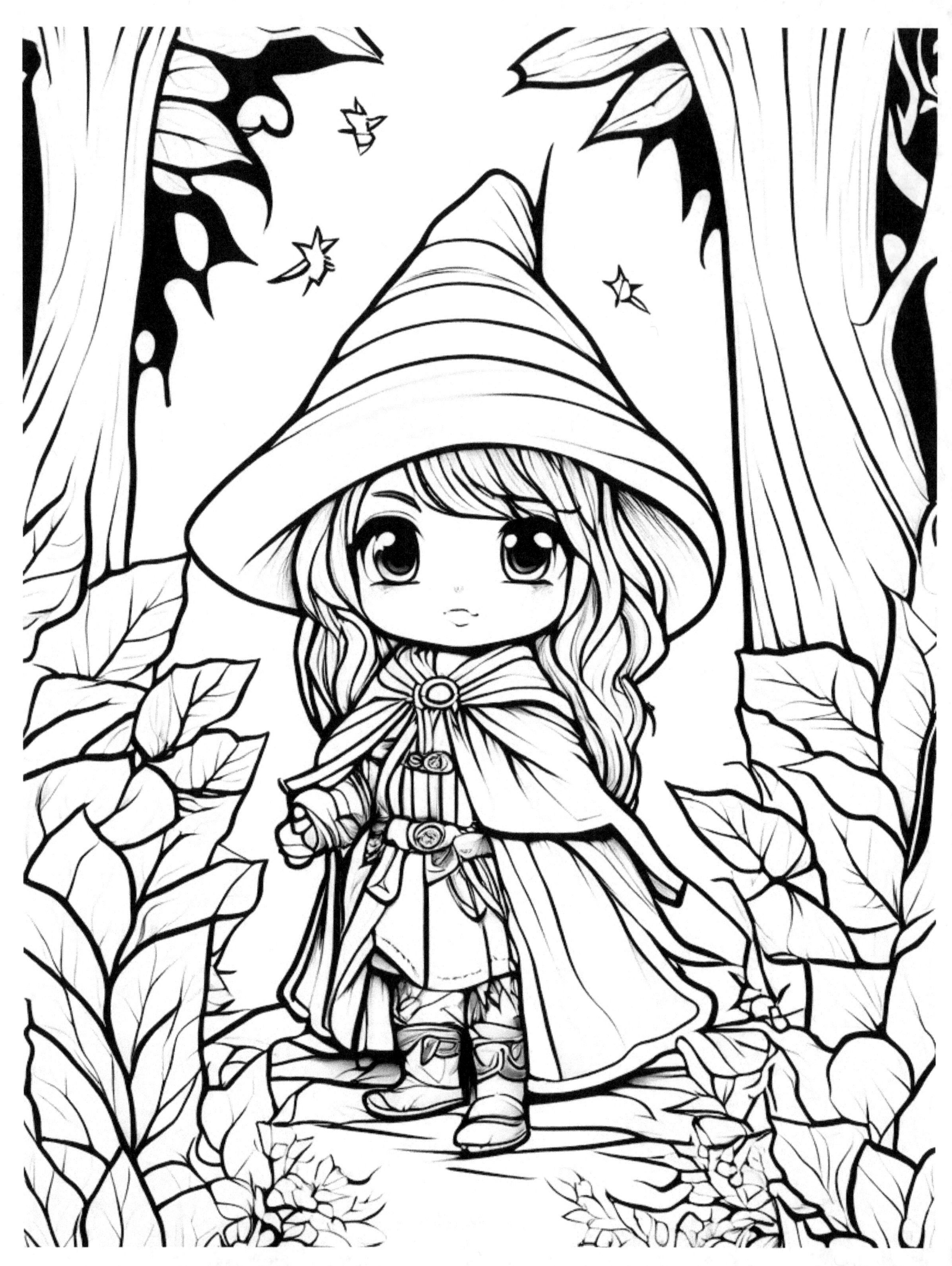

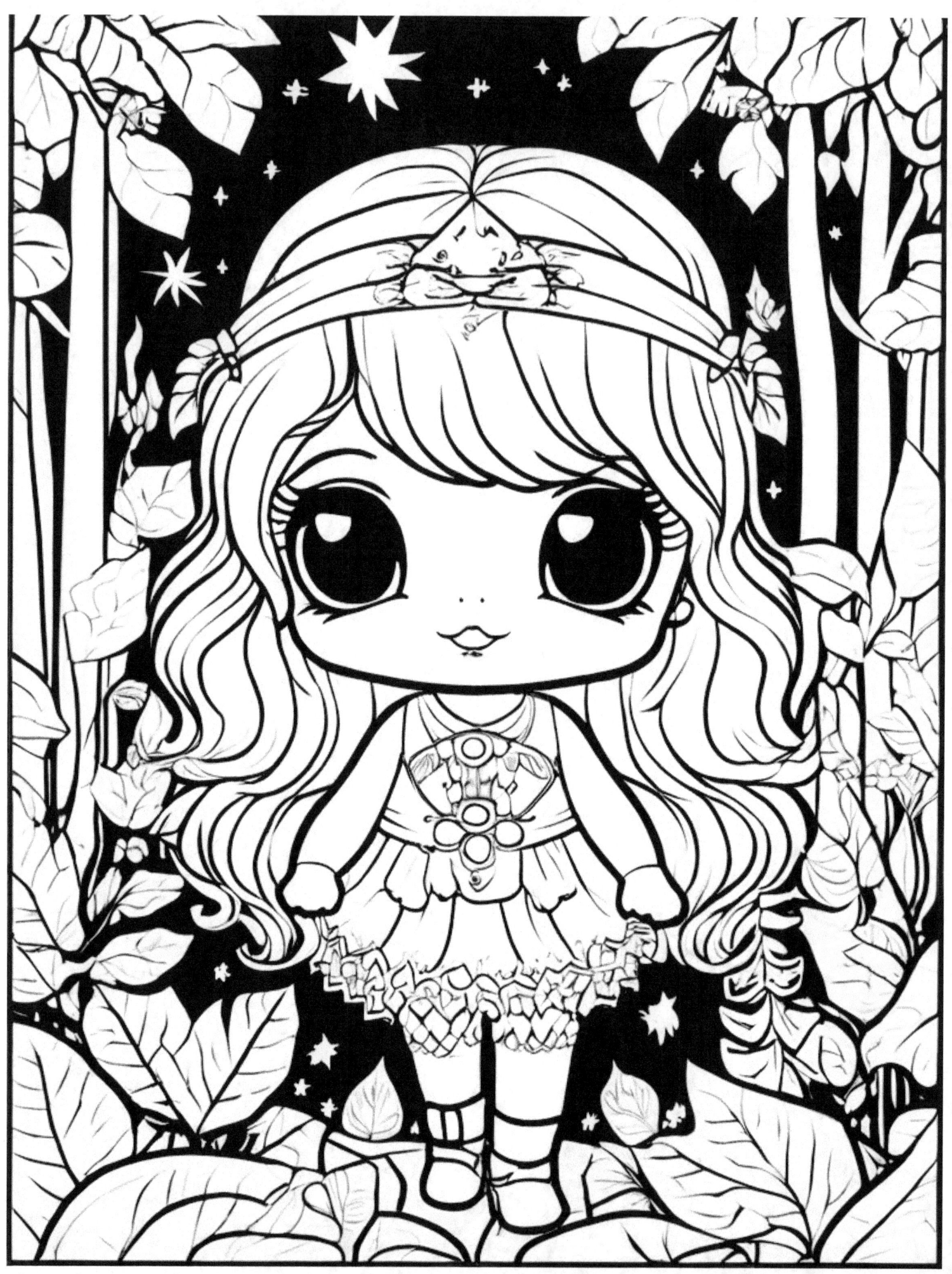

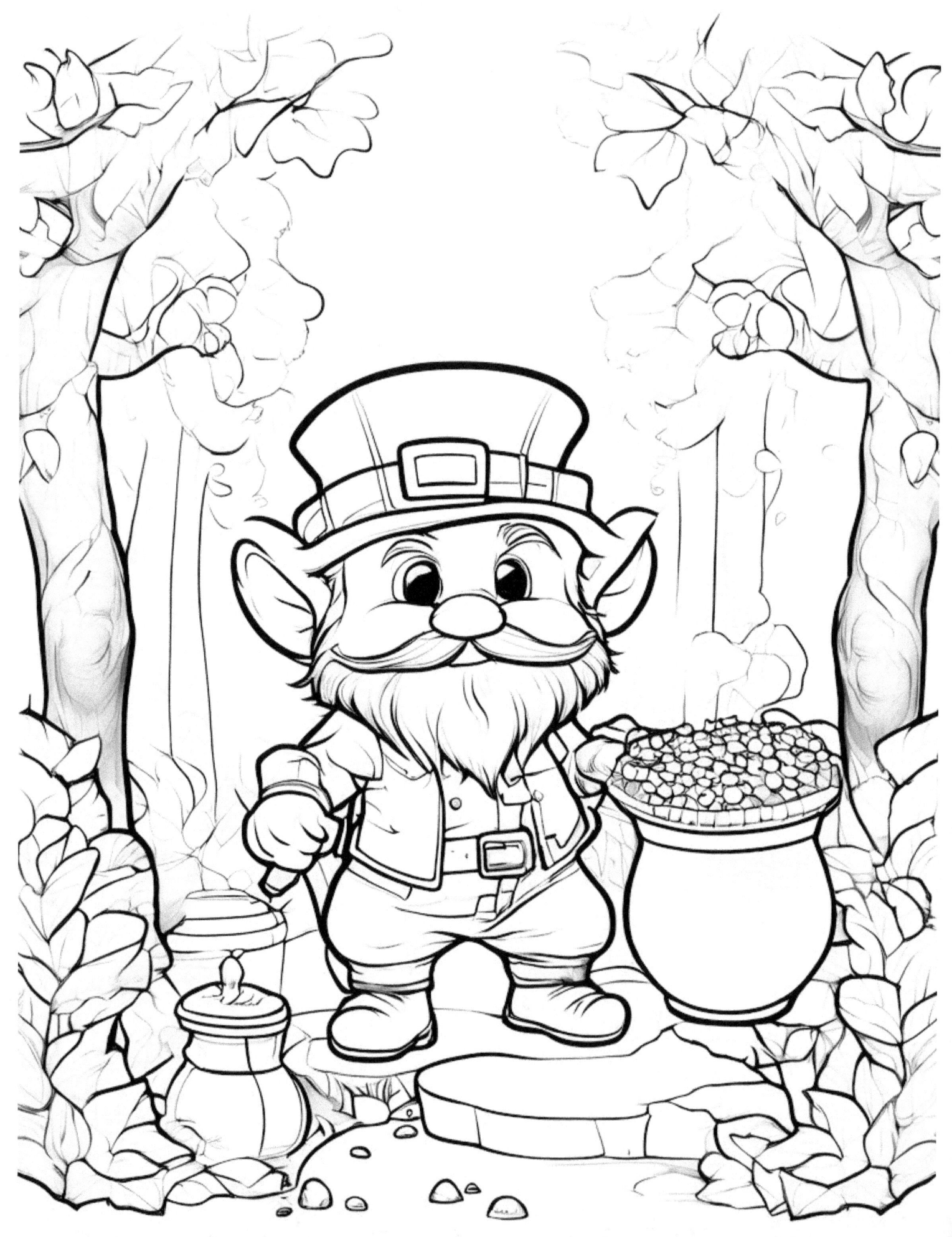

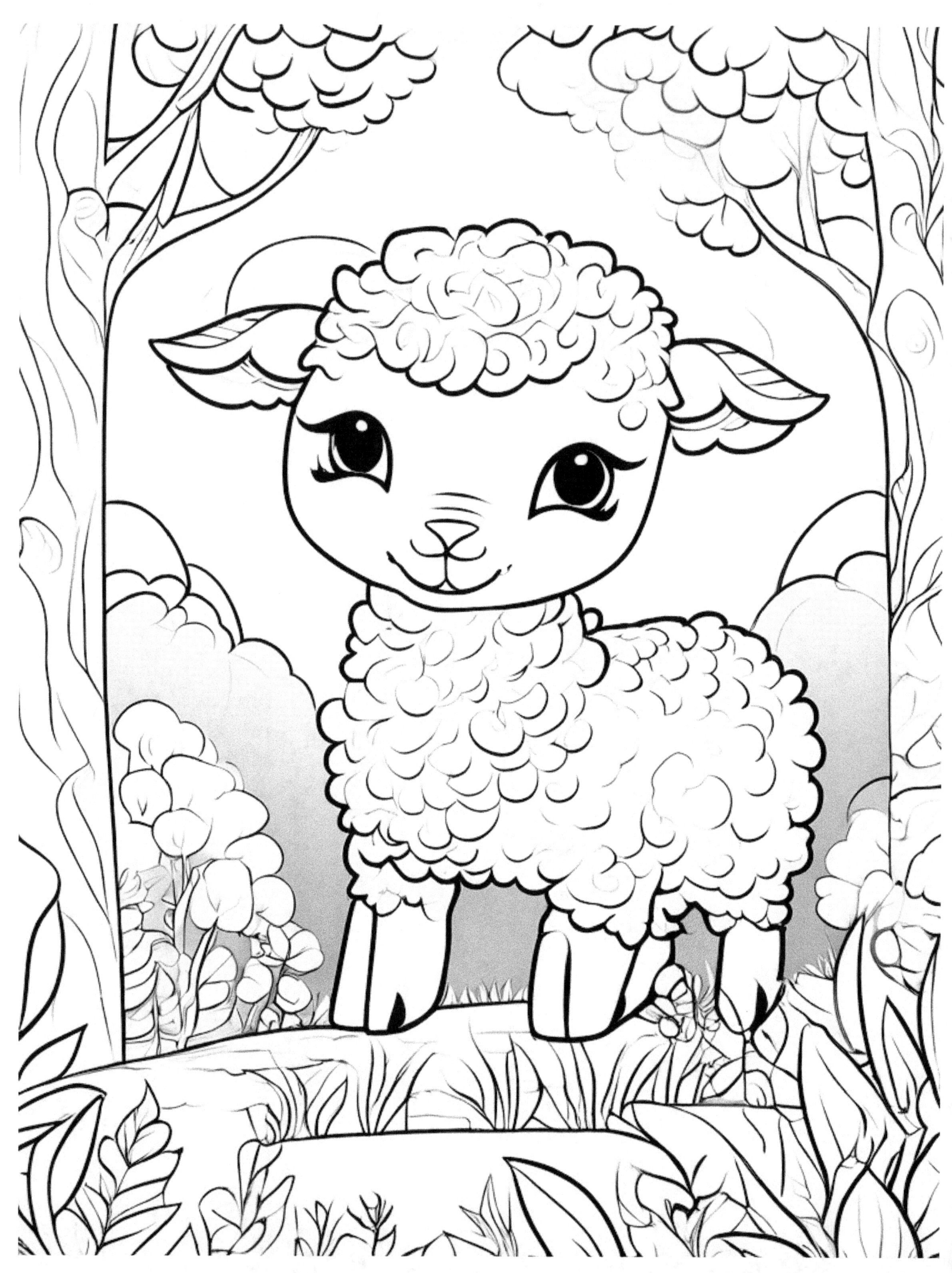

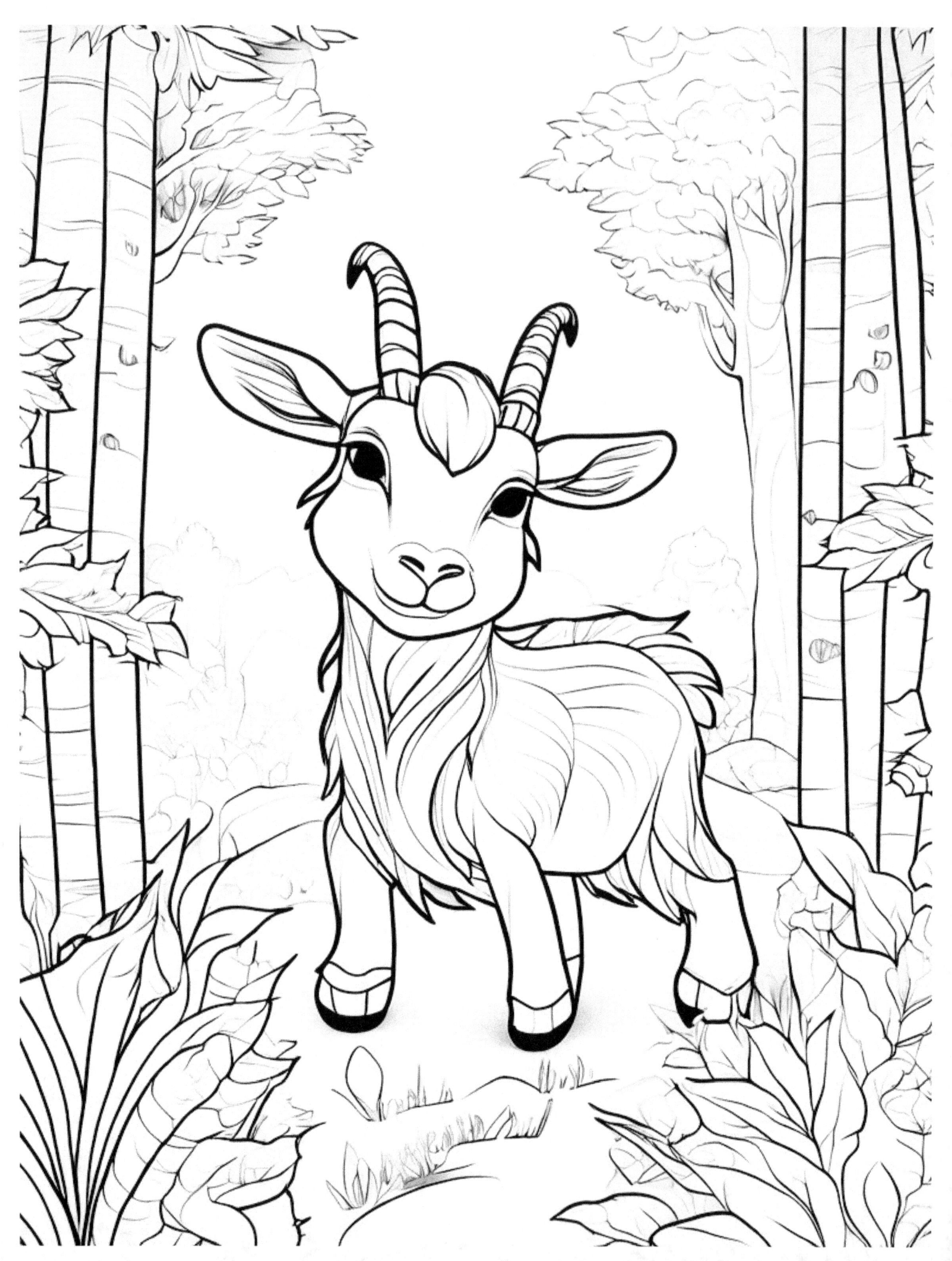

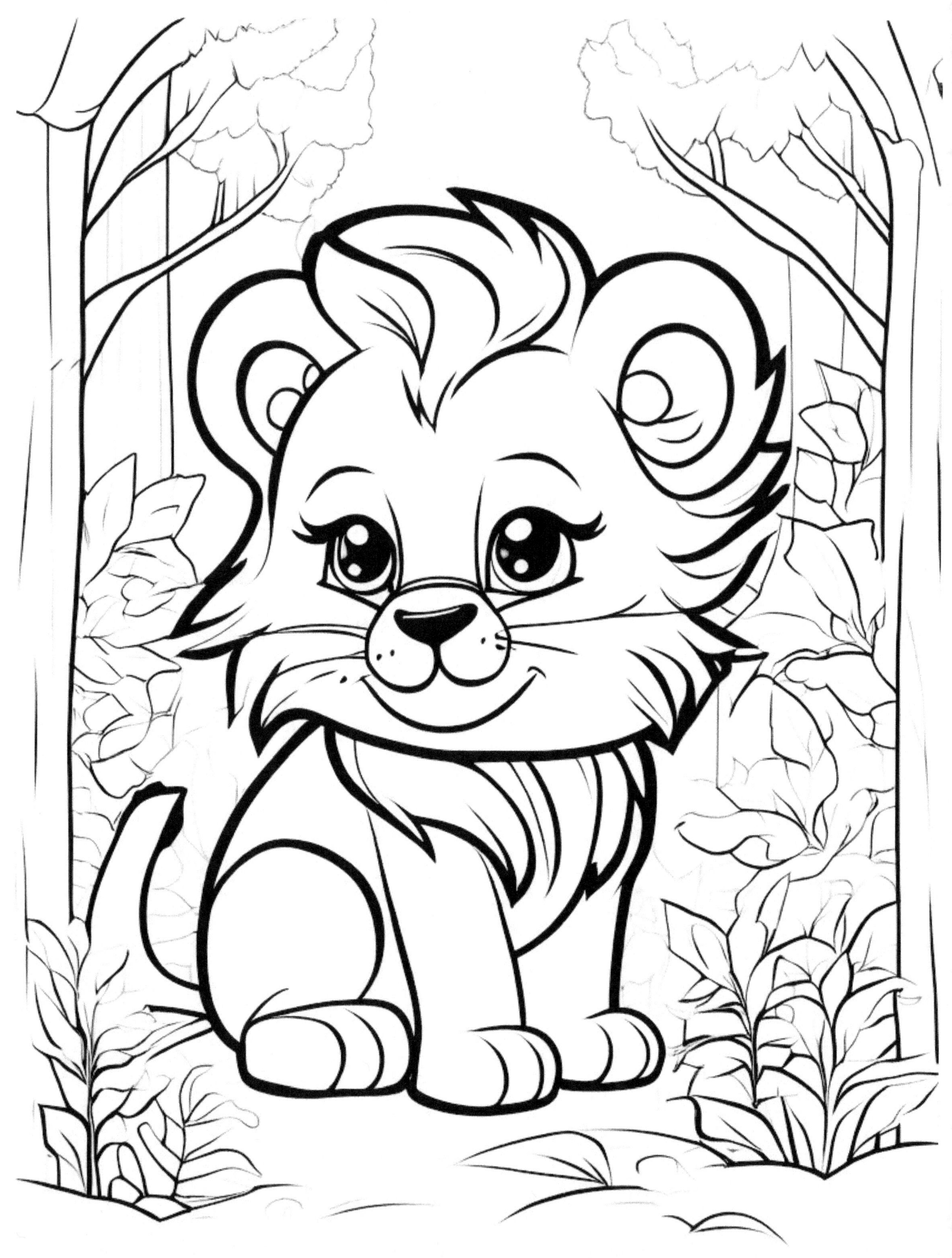

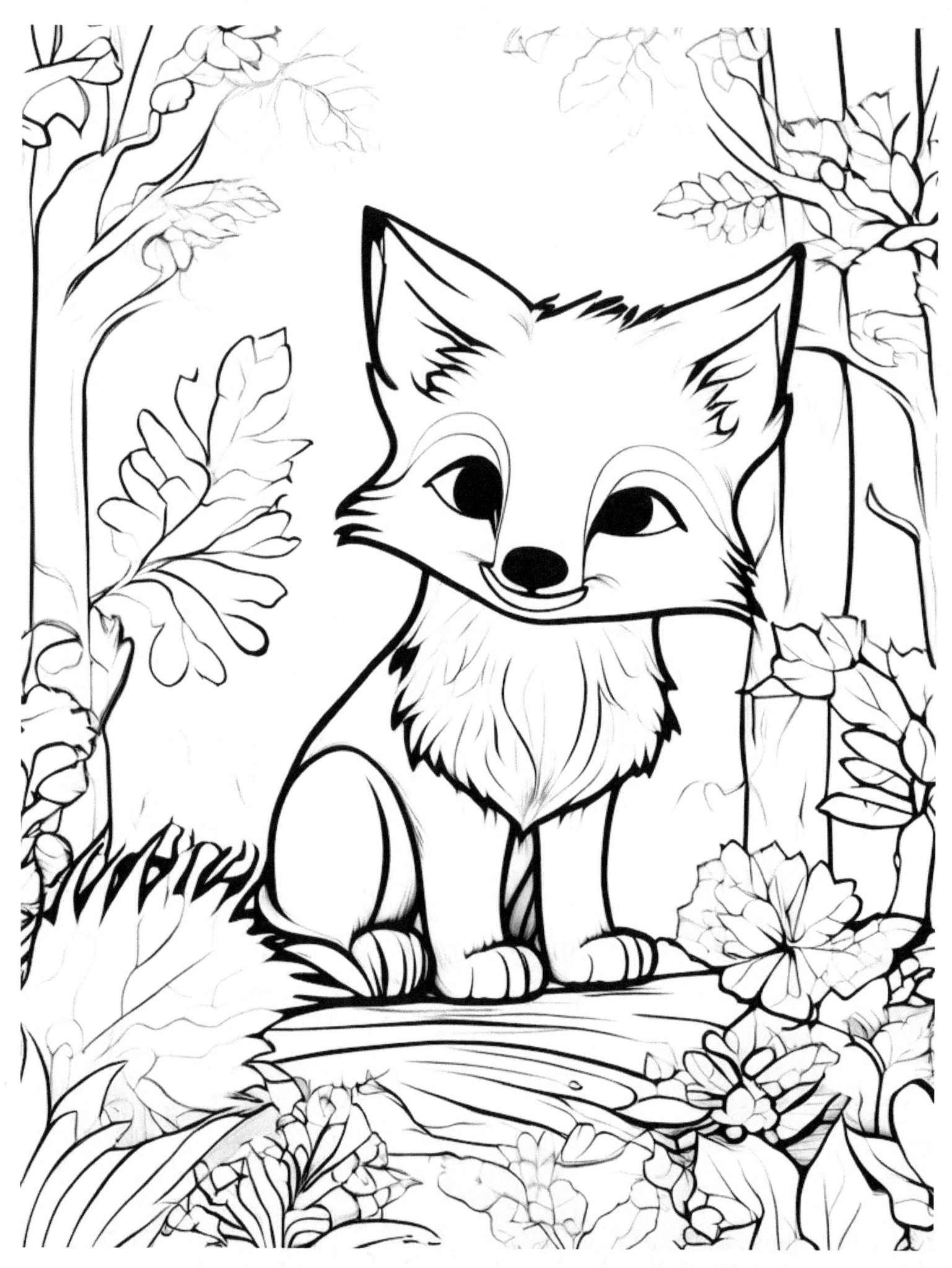

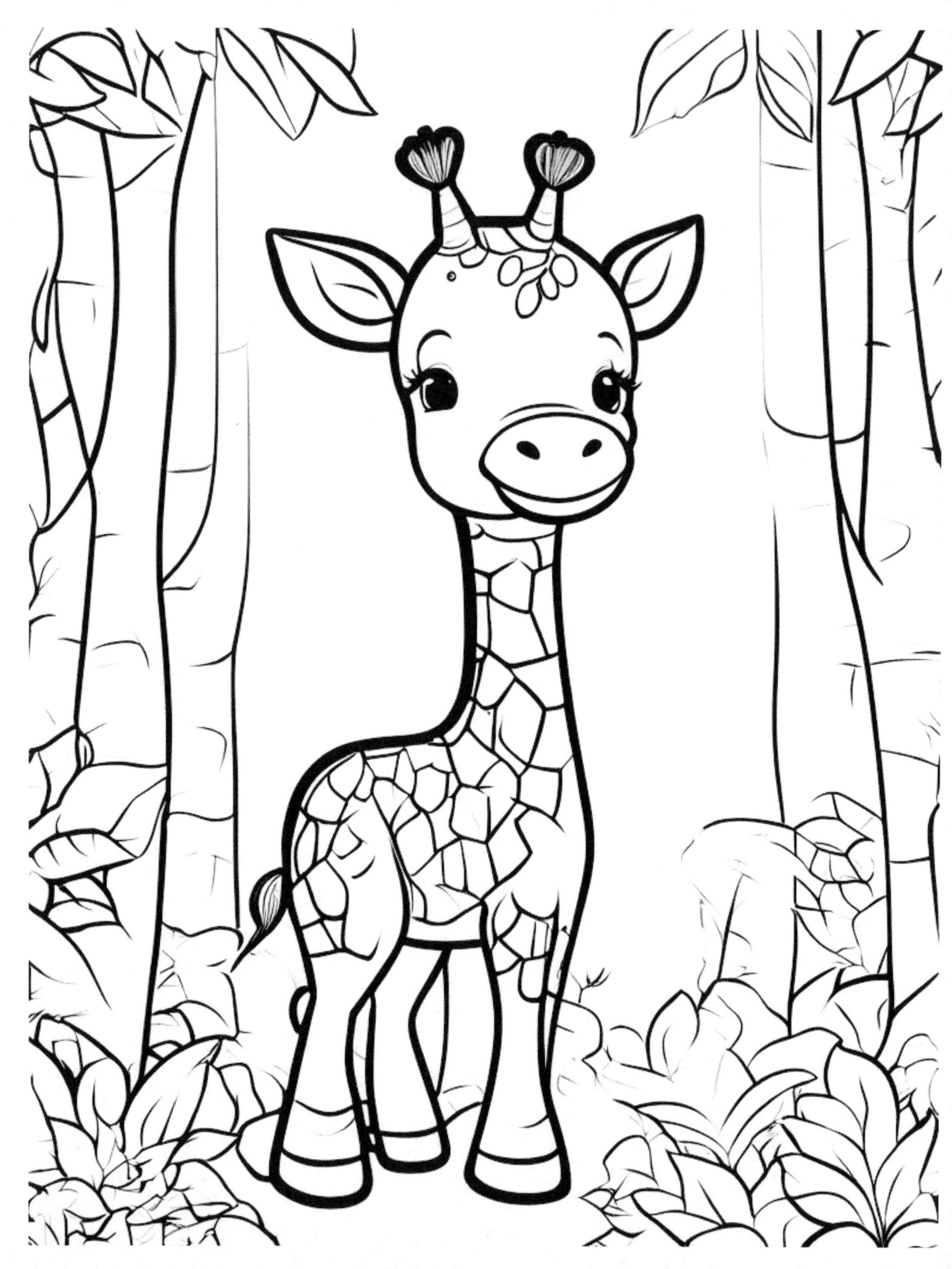

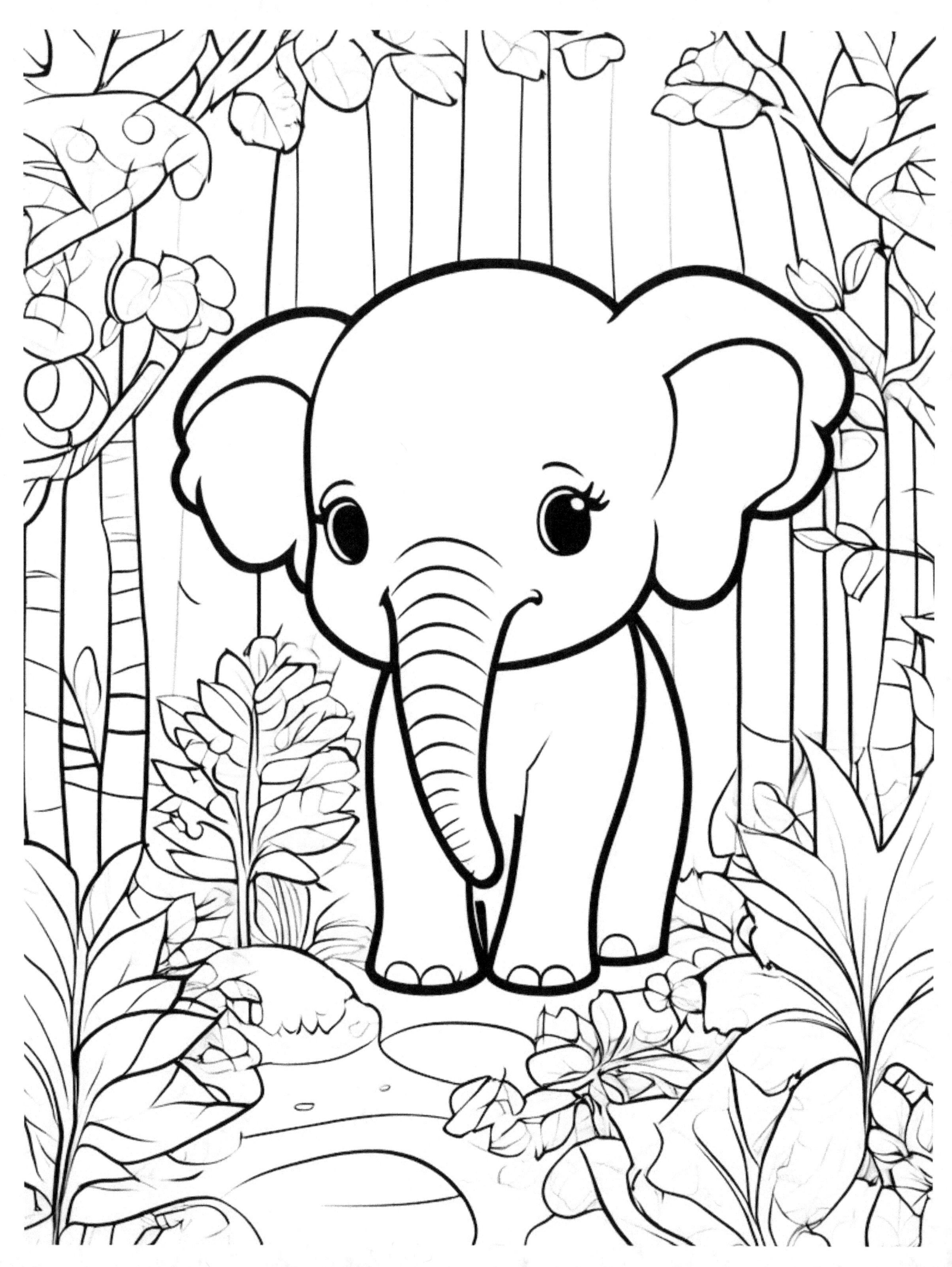

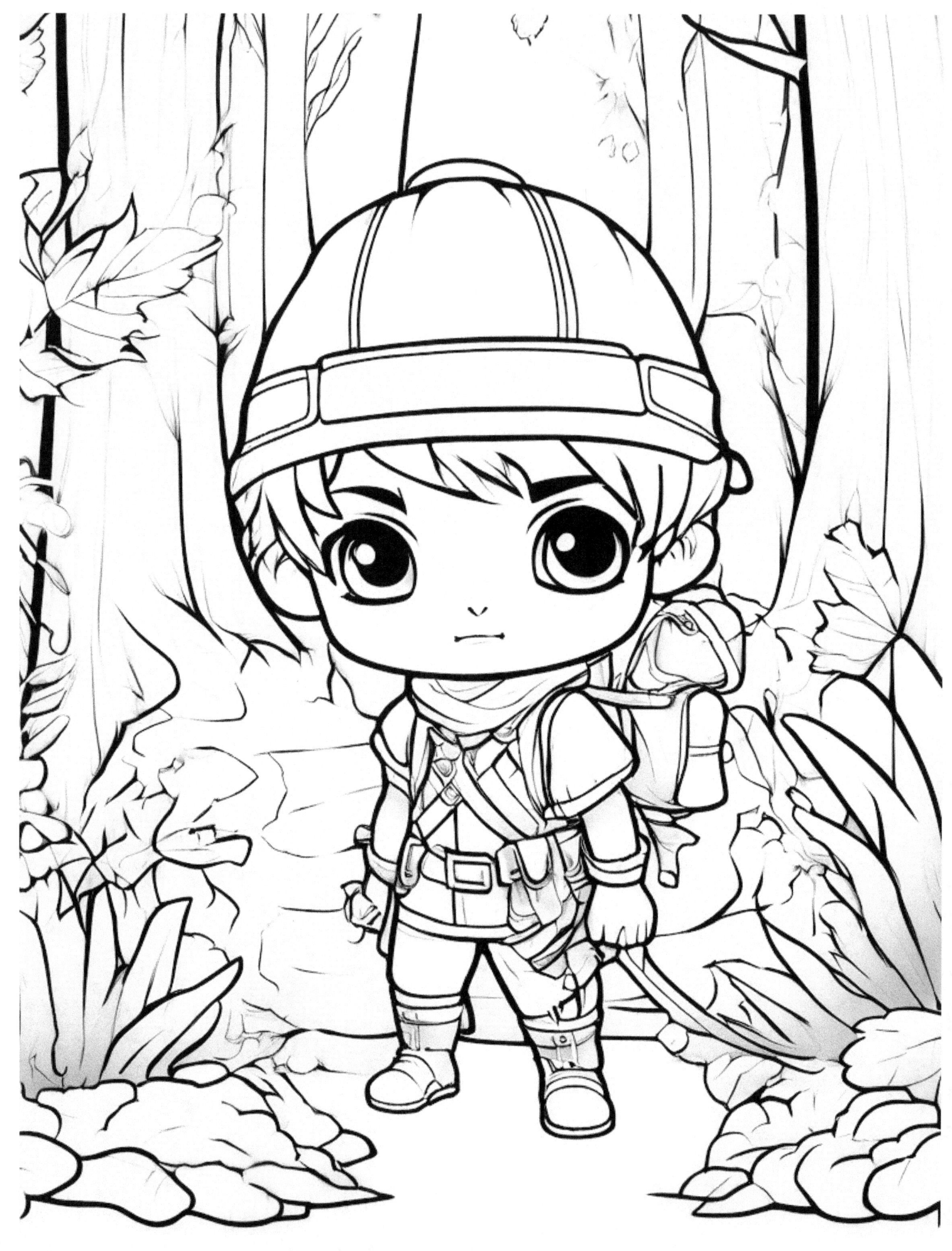

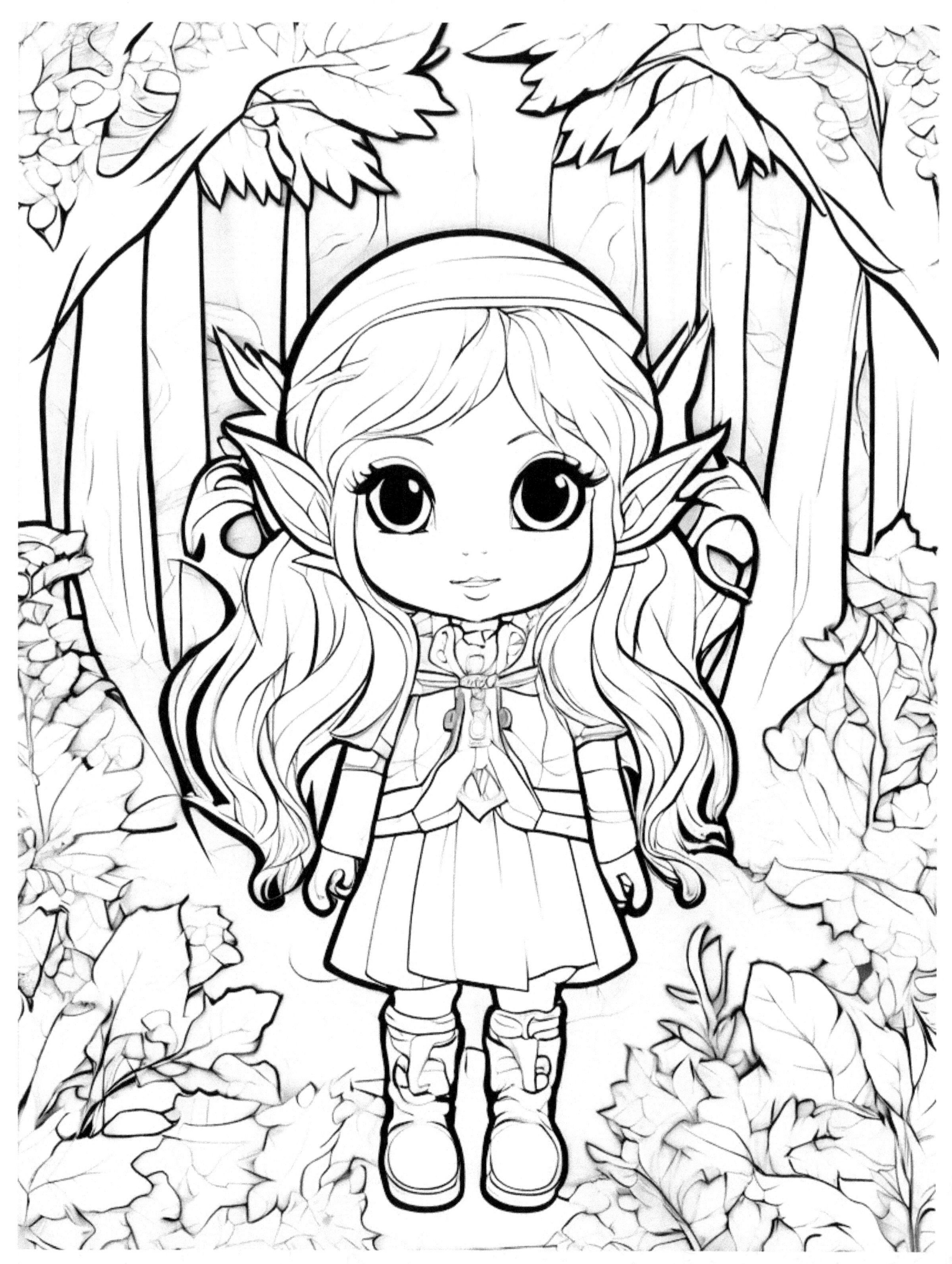

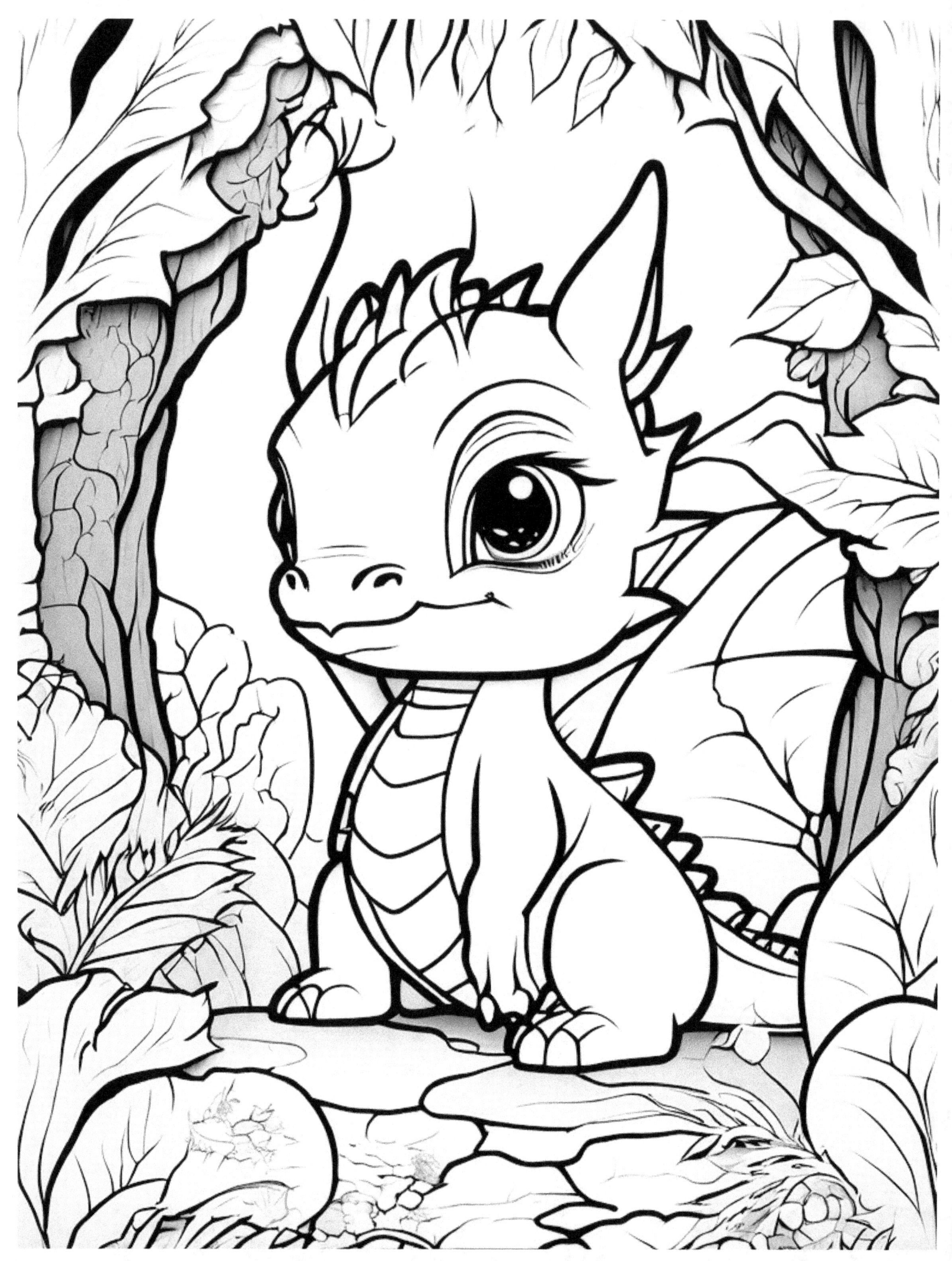

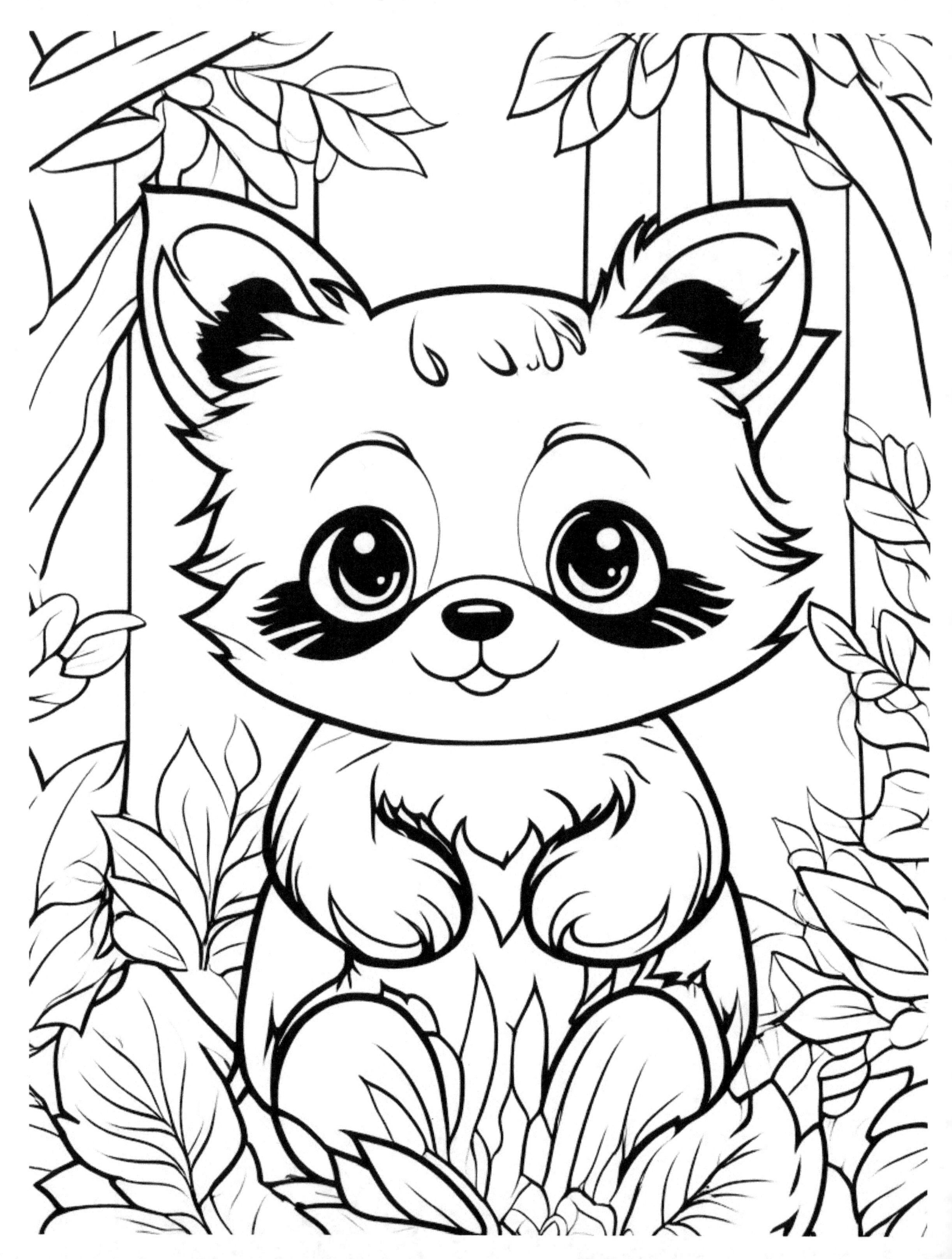

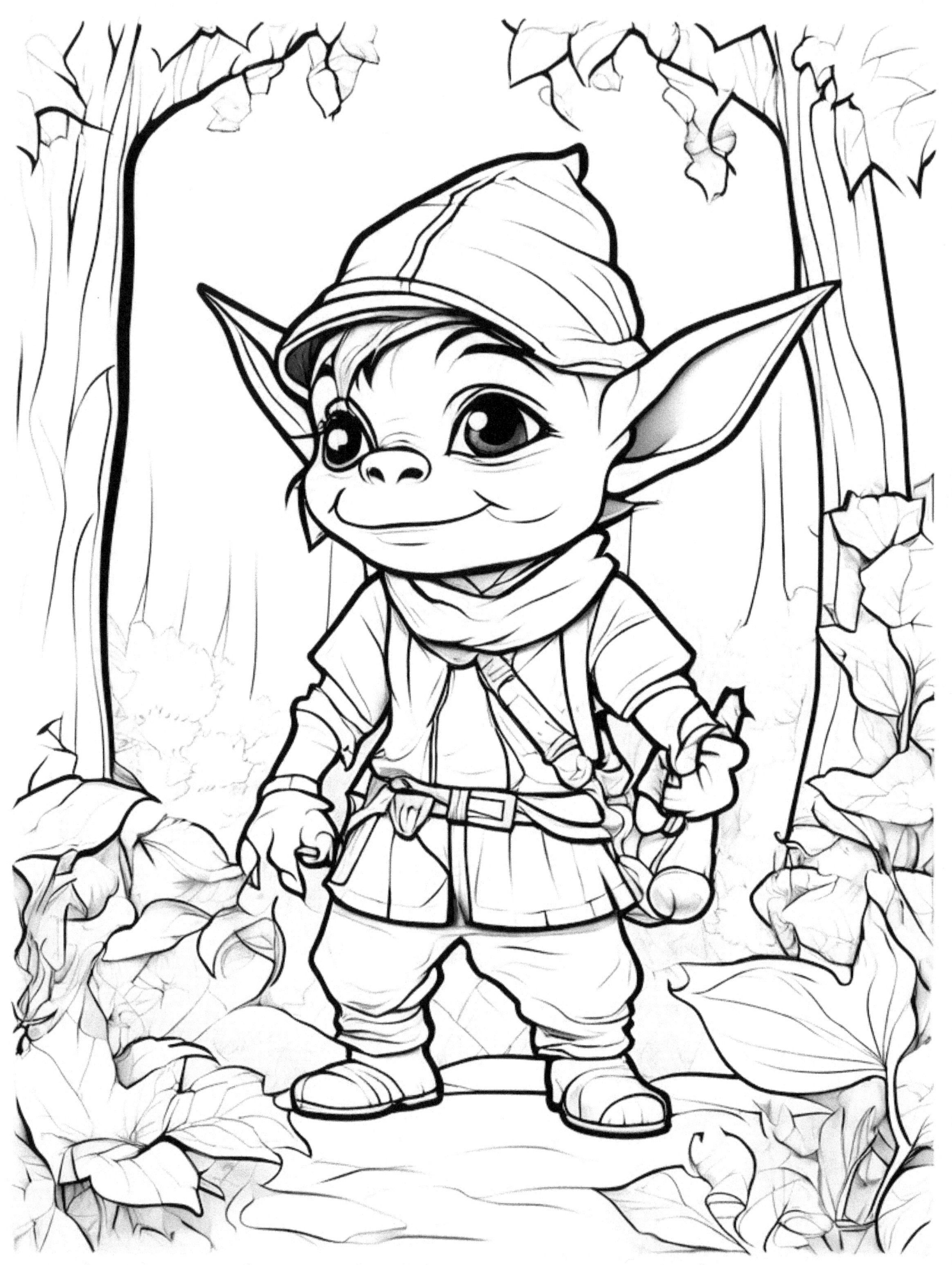

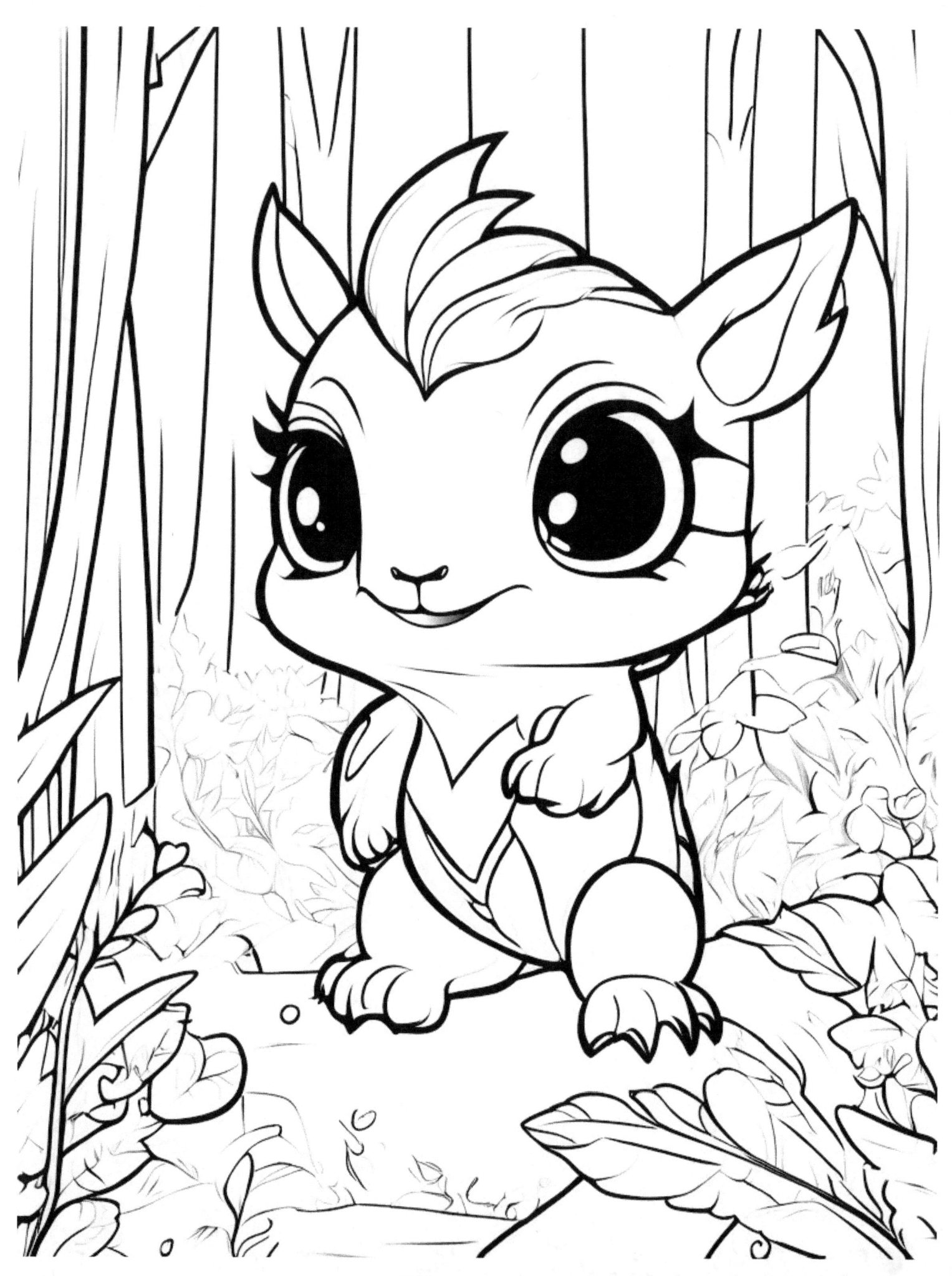

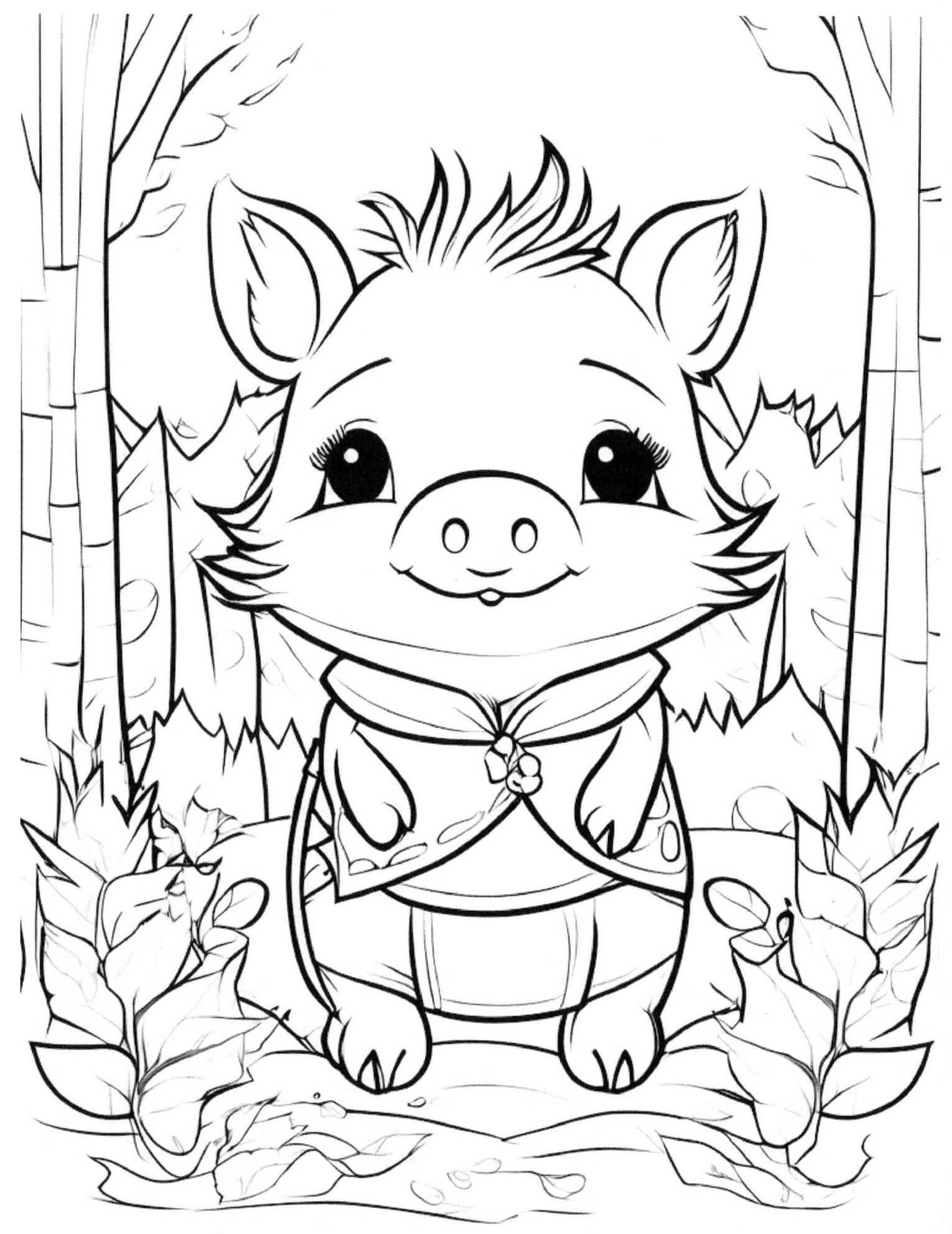

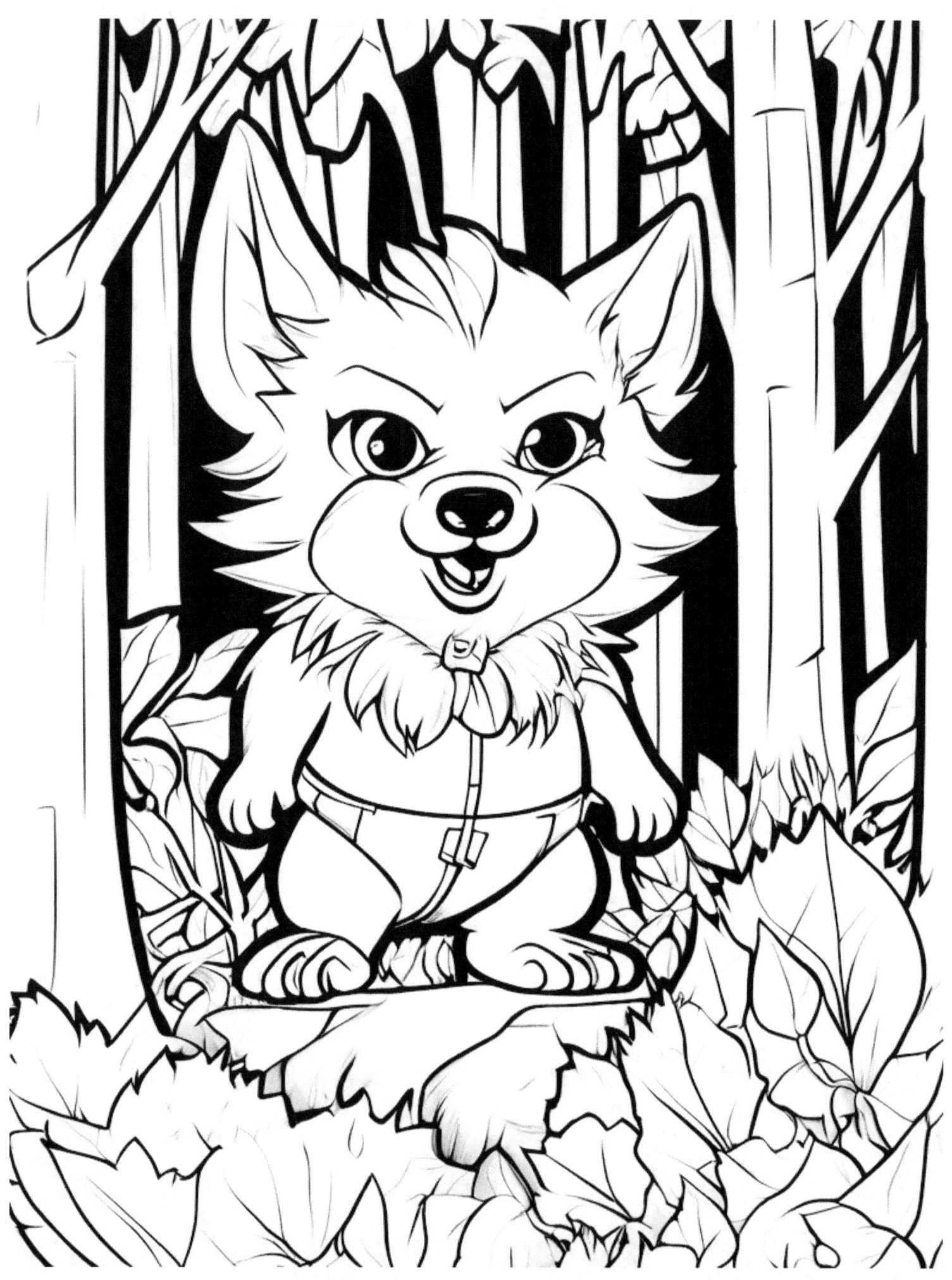

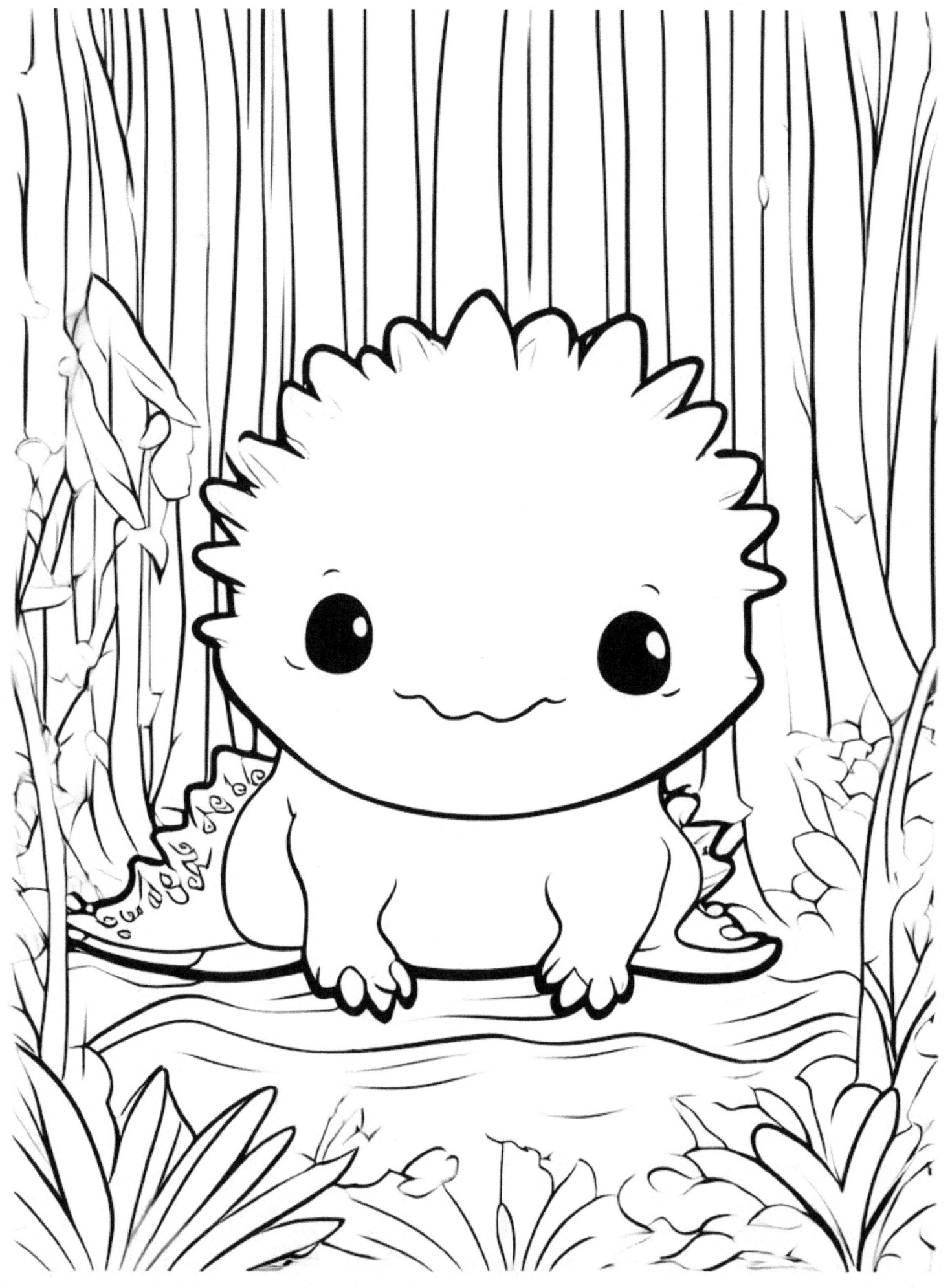

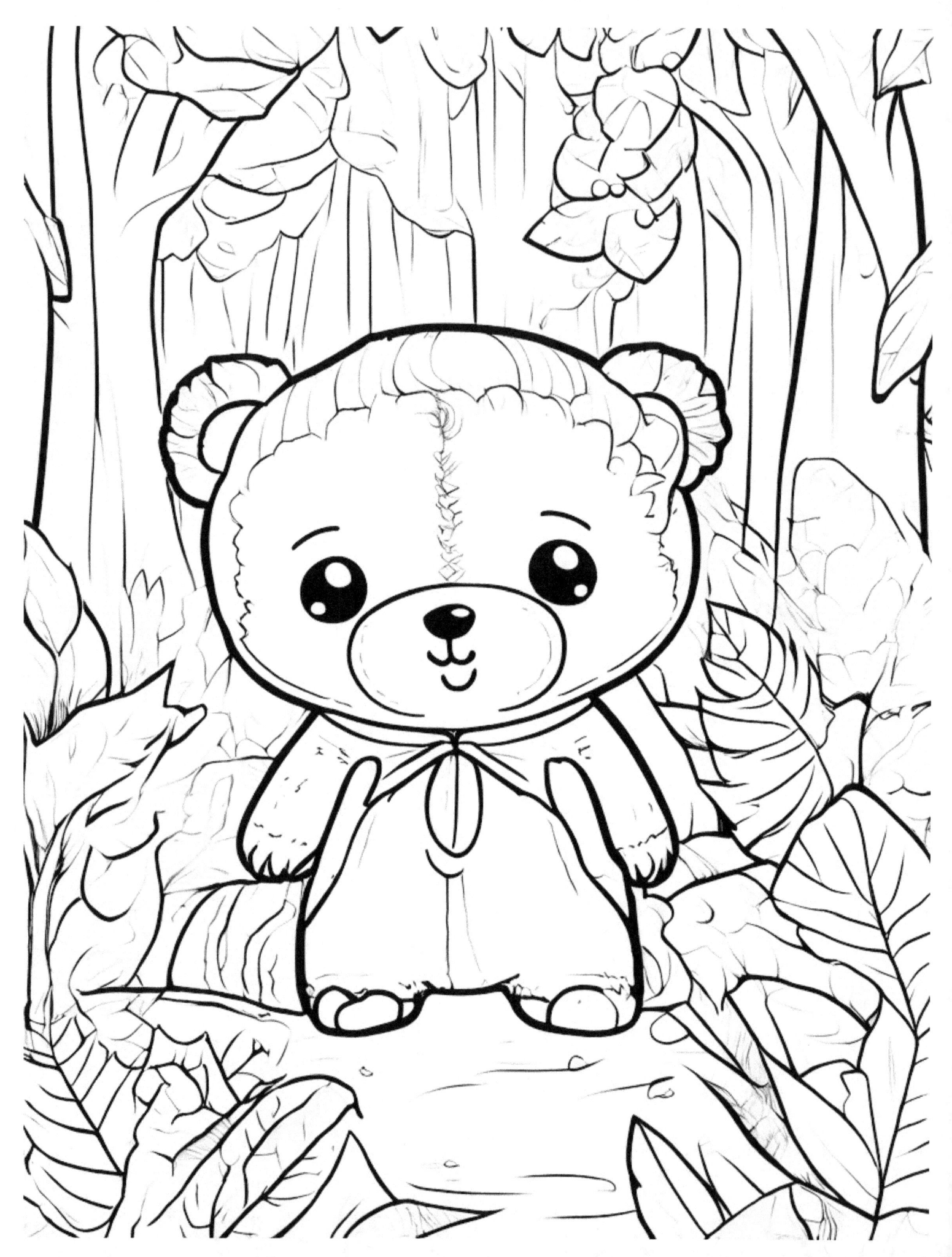

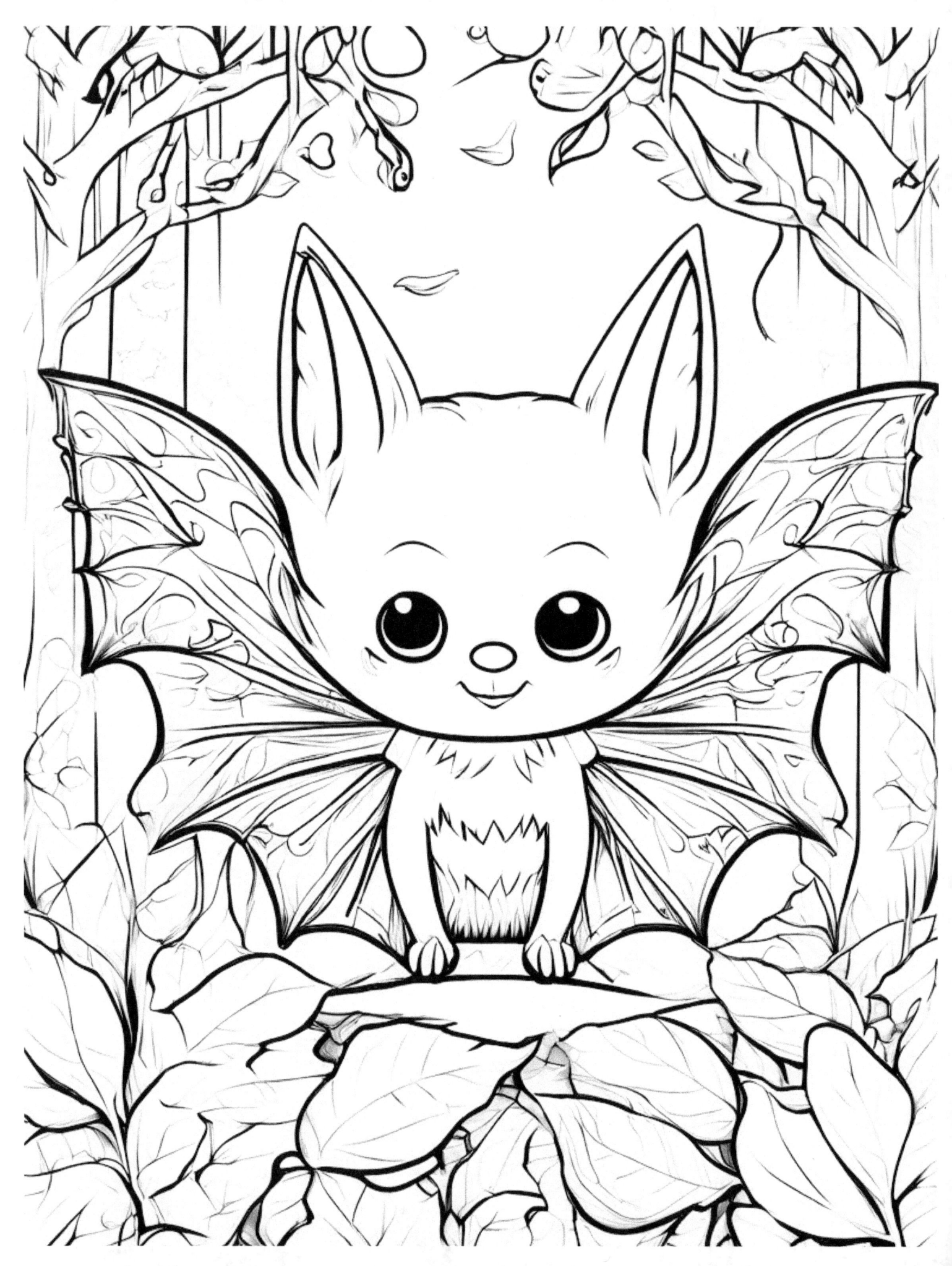